Henry James

Henry James

The

Crooked

Corridor

Elizabeth Stevenson
with a new introduction by the author

Transaction Publishers
New Brunswick (U.S.A.) and London (U.K.)

Library of Congress Catalog Number: 00-023379
ISBN: 0-7658-0694-0
Printed in the United States of America

Library of Congress Cataloging-in-Publication Data

Stevenson, Elizabeth, 1919-1999
    Henry James : the crooked corridor / Elizabeth Stevenson.
        p. cm.
    Originally published : The crooked corridor : a study of Henry James.
    New York : Macmillian, 1949. With new introduction.
    ISBN 0-7658-0694-0 (alk. paper)
    1. James, Henry, 1843-1916.   2. Authors, American—19th century—
Biography. I. Title.

PS2123 . S8 2000
813' .4—dc21
[B]   00-023379

To my father
John Thurman Stevenson

Contents

Introduction to the Transaction Edition

IT HAS BEEN EASY FOR SOME READERS AND CRITICS TO DENIGRATE HENRY James for two contradictory reasons. He has been thought a writer limited in his scope and depth in his treatment of a certain class of people. On the other hand, adding to the puzzlement, he has been thought to be too complex, too extreme in putting into difficult wordage his view of the relationships between his chosen characters.

But Henry James stands there, a stout and strong presence in the literature of the English language, from the relatively youthful, straightforward, and simple writing of his early years to the involved complexities of his later stories. He cannot be denied. There seems to me to have been a misunderstanding in the minds of those who make the objections. It is true nearly all of his characters are well clothed, well fed, and roofed comfortably. They are usually fairly well educated and talk literately and wittily. He rarely treats raw or wild nature, but he is sensitive to landscape as a background.

There are interesting exceptions to this description. He does children well, and they are often outside the norms of society. Who can forget Daisy Miller's nasty little brother? Who is not touched by the uncanny in the tainted children of *The Turn of the Screw*, whether the taint is actually in the children or in the mind of the governess? He does writers and painters and those of that ilk very well, because he was one of them. But their views cannot be taken into the norm of society even if sometimes they conform in their behavior. James was "well-behaved," but his mind ranged beyond the comfortable and the accepted.

In one novel, *The Princess Casamassima*, he took up seriously the underside of London life. In Paul Muniment, he painted with cruel precision, the single-minded, heartless reformer who did not care what he made of others in order to achieve his end. James had been listening to his sister, Alice, who was emotionally a political and social radical. The book was never well received by critical opinion, but I have found it interesting and appealing, with its almost Dickensian beginning in the scene of a small, frightened boy being taken to visit with his mother in a dank prison, where she is confined for murdering her lover. And the climax of this book hangs upon a promise of the hero's to commit a political assassination, when called upon.

But stories such as *The Princess* are simply exceptions to James' normal writing occupation, a concern with the appetites and compulsions of individuals living the supposed good life. James had gifts that make these stories go. There is always a plot. Something always *happens*. Behind the surface of life there is always drama, even melodrama. Told in bare detail, his tales could be pure soap opera. But he is concerned deeply otherwise. His writing is not an impression, although it is that indeed; and it is not simply a skillful engineering of happenings. It is an original kind of exploration of the heights and depths of the human mind.

There is a doubleness about his presentation. He shows you the act. Then he makes you understand the mind of the actor. In these tragic stories (nearly always tragic, although James was master of a certain kind of observant humor), we know the deepest emotions that drive the human heart.

The way he gets you into these dramas is always interesting. In *The Ambassadors*, he hooks you as a viewer, almost as a partaker, more and more involved. How long, you wonder, will it be until Lambert Strether sees the truth of the relationships between Chad and Marie de Vionnet? In this case, you as a reader are ahead of Strether. You see not only Chad change, but Lambert Strether too—the "ambassador" sent out by Chad's mother to bring a bad boy home from the wiles of a foreign woman. As he observes the two whose relationships, he thinks, must break up, he, the observer, changes too. For this older American realizes how much in life he has missed, and finds that this European experience opens up a new world to him. He sees that it has been a beneficence to the younger man, changing him from a raw youth into a civilized human being. And he sees further: Marie is a worthy, suffering person, deeply caring for

Chad. And Chad has not the sensitivity to value this love enough. He shows Chad's essential vulgarity in rejecting Marie's love for convenience, gain, and position back home.

In *The Wings of the Dove*, Milly's nobility shines as she realizes that she has been betrayed by Kate Croy, her best friend, and Merton Dansher, her aspiring lover and one expectant to be her husband. Kate has persuaded Merton to cause Milly to love him when the two of them discover she is dying. Milly is an incredibly wealthy, single, beautiful American "princess." If Merton Densher, pushed into this by Kate Croy, should marry Milly before the disease carries her off, then, after her death, the two of them will be rich. (You see how melodramatic the events alone are.)

It is after her death, after she has turned her face to the wall, after she has refused to see Merton Densher and Kate Croy again—having learned of their scheme— but left her money to them; then the schemers wake up to their own damnation. "We shall never again be to each other as we were!"

Betrayal, for James, is the greatest sin; and a kind of non-churchly renunciation of self-interest is a virtue.

Isabel Archer, in *The Portrait of a Lady*, steps out of the pages of the book on the way to Rome where trouble awaits her attempts to rescue Pansy, her stepdaughter, from schemes of her husband, Gilbert Osmond, the girl's father. He is determined to marry her "well," to someone she does not love.

If, in James, one does not travel physically a great deal, except to the resorts of those well-off financially and socially, one travels extensively through the minds and hearts of his characters.

Re-reading James this time, I admit that he is difficult. And one might want, in certain moods, a more direct approach. But the journey rewards the traveler. I find I say again: he is worth it. The delicacy of his "melodramatic" insights causes a tremor or appreciation from a reader: yes, this is the way life is, this is true, both horrible and wonderful. And no one else has expressed this understanding in this way.

Elizabeth Stevenson

PART One

The Man

THE BENT BACK OF A MAN WRITING IS NOT THE MOST CHARAC-
teristic image of the years between the American Civil
War and the First World War. That attitude was the characteristic one of Henry James during those years which were the
years of his maturity. The man was the artist: he had no other
function than as an observant, reflective, productive imagination. This quiet fact alienated him from his own time. That
period's great men were explorers of gross facts and empty areas,
exploiters, builders of nations and empires, reformers, and system makers. Such men became the symbols of the age. Our symbols are not those of the nineteenth century. In the revolution
that has afflicted and changed us, the conscious, feeling, private
individual has again become significant. The twentieth century,
in revulsion, has turned from the public man to the private
man. Such an individual James was. Although his works do not
require the commentary of his life, his existence itself was a
comment upon his age.

He was born in New York on April 15, 1843. He died on Feb-
ruary 28, 1916, in London, after living almost seventy-three
years. The life that he lived during those years has only an ironical bearing upon the great public events of the time. While he
was a child, the covered wagons moved westward to Oregon and
California. In France, Louis Napoleon became Napoleon III.
Italians and Germans prepared their loosely united countrymen for nationalism and war. In England the Chartists marched

densely and hopelessly in London's streets, parading for the workingman's right to vote. At the age of seventeen, the boy heard the report of John Brown's raid on the army installation at Harper's Ferry. The war which broke the country in half found him old enough to catch the full force of the impression. With the war past and a decision made, he went to live in Europe. He became a stranger to America during the digging, building years of growth after the Civil War. The rude magnificence of the seventies and eighties and nineties, the spewing up of robber barons, money kings, trust makers and busters, all the struggling, constructive, fighting era would necessarily find an author of the inner life beside the point. And, in return, the author would find the facts of public existence little to his purpose. He lived, thereafter, in Italy, in France, and more continually, in England. But in the Europe of tightening nationalisms, of rivalries for sea lanes and colonies, he was essentially as lonely as he had been in America. However, he was granted there, as a matter of course, the negative privilege of being left alone to practice his trade. Toward the end of his life, the World War, the unimaginable catastrophe, caught him up into active correspondence with public life. The war killed the old man as effectively as it killed many young men.

As James knew, it is the personal life that is rich. Subjective passion, translated into objects, that is, stories and novels, worked within him upon a thousand relations and ramifications of intense living. These experiences were his own affair then, and some of great importance necessarily remain unknown. However, the sense of life vibrates in the works. Our age has a legitimate curiosity about that life. The few circumstances which are to be touched upon in the following paragraphs are the obvious ones, and certainly not all. But each one discussed has a subterranean connection with the work as well as an interest of its own, for James shaped an individual existence which has, in perspective, as definite a form as one of his stories.

Each connection to be traced, then, between life and work, opens a window upon the study of the work. But more, it opens a window upon the need of the present time, for sound individuals, pursuing private work. It is in the latter sense that we look for connections rather than from any absolute need to explain his work by his environment. They cannot be explained by anything outside them. They exist as complete worlds. With this preliminary, one can tick off quickly the list of peculiar circumstances, the facts of the man's life, which seem necessary to complete or to make the kind of man he was: family, education, an injured back, the study of drawing, "Europe," travel, London and success, the retirement to Rye, unpopularity, playwrighting, or what he called his "sawdust and orange-peel phase," the return to America in 1904 and 1905, illness, the war, and death.

The list above is the essential one. Each fact, in turn, sent circles out upon his imagination which spent seventy-three years refining, altering, disguising, using these facts and making them over into independent forms.

Freedom anchored incorruptibly in security: this was the family. "We wholesomely breathed inconsistency and ate and drank contradictions," said James of himself and his brothers and sister. William and Henry, who was the second son, Wilky, Bob, and Alice were the unspoiled children of this inconsistency and freedom. The fact of growing up in such a family reverberates through the author's life. It gave him a point of reference and the unconscious courage of always being himself. It gave him the unarguable right to the bent of his own imagination.

To have had an unworldly father and to have heard mysticism discussed at the family dinner table are advantages that most novelists of the civilized society can hardly have shared with Henry James. His father, Henry James, Sr., who had inherited enough money from his merchant father to please himself, stayed home and wrote books which were honored by the indifference of his age, and brought up a family which was an exception to the rule of the American society of that time in not being in the least exposed to business. The children, four boys and a girl, were exposed to much more beguiling and dangerous interests, those of religion, science, pleasure, and art. Henry, later, when he saw how different his childhood had been from any other he ever observed, thought that it had been quaint to have begun rather than evolved into the inner life.

Around this odd circle was the "small warm dusky, homogeneous New York world of the mid-century." Up the river and beyond the city was a vague circle of uncles and aunts and cousins who were known to be "wild," the merchant's money not having always agreed with second- and third-generation Jameses. Beyond, the expanse of America loomed, with only the shadow of Daniel Webster to give it a political shape. Within doors was the philosopher father, who made the spiritual as familiar and merry as the postman's ring, and the mother in whom they all, father and children, simply rested.

"Father's Ideas," which the child knew to be religious but not connected with any church, all tended to show that everything was one, while his son's in turn were to tend to show that there were very many irreducible elements which of necessity ground against each other. Yet the striking difference of their sense of life cannot diminish the importance for the second Henry James of his having lived with a man of his father's mental distinction.

The great point of his childhood was that he was allowed to be. What he was was nothing very distinguished. But although Henry could not seem to be anything at first but vague, he could be so without compunction, vague and receptive and dumb. On the other hand, William, the perpetual older brother, guided his own course, even as a boy, with a masterful hand. He could grow into his broad scientific and philosophic distinction by stepping easily from drawing to collecting to dissecting to teaching without surprising Henry, who hung back and admired William. It was strange, but in the pattern of their childhood, that Henry could always read William, but that William, as the years went on, could less and less read Henry and could send Henry an unmerciful objection to a novel quite in the popular, philistine line of criticism.

Environment seems to have been powerless to prevent the diametrically opposite growth of two powerful natures: William's toward the experimental, Henry's toward the imaginative and synthesizing. Henry understood their inherent differences perfectly and stated them as the gap between one's caring for, "visibly provoked or engineered phenomena," and caring for, "the mysteriously or insidiously aggressive, the ambushed or suffered sort."

The schooling which Henry shared with William, with William always upstairs, a year or so ahead, was of the most haphazard kind. Its importance for Henry was entirely negative. No schooling could help and none could hurt too much, so long as it left the brooding faculty free. During these years, the two boys attended numberless boys' schools, both in America and in Europe, devoted variously to accounting, to algebra and physics, at which Henry was hardly more than an idiot, or to French conversation. At a more appropriate academy in Geneva, Henry amused himself by pretending that the lectures on literature were a species of comedy and those on science, tragedy. He was happily relieved by special arrangement from taking any examinations. He had, after all, the type of mind that could take up a relationship to a fact only after his imagination had worked to transform that fact.

The sights of the streets, the hotels and theaters of his childhood were more directly transformable by that faculty and of even greater importance as education. These entertainments of the mind were city entertainments. The James children were always, "very towny and domesticated little persons," who knew nothing of country life and whose "salon was mainly the street, loose and rude and crude in those days at best."

One of the schools he remembered best allowed the boys, in the absence of the scientific, sanitary playground, the freedom of lower Broadway. Street sights and sounds educated. He remembered, later, the red danger flags of the workers who were building the early subways, and the adventure it was to skirt the area where momentarily the explosion of rock and earth was expected. He remembered the simpler, smellier docksides of that day, the open-air piles of fruit, the cobblestones on which the horse-drawn drays lurched high and dangerous. He remembered ferry rides with his father and one particular day's adventure, the going with his father for a photograph of them to be made by the great Mr. Brady in his Broadway studio, and standing stiffly beside him. The picture, surviving today, testifies to Brady's patient solidity of perception.

Everything outside school and home was an innocent excess of freedom that never seemed to hurt: streets, hotels, an oddity of churches, theaters, and circuses. William rebuffed Henry one day with, "I play with boys who curse and swear!" and Henry, admitting that as yet he didn't, was relegated to a far-wandering freedom of walks, which seem to have been allowed the younger boy on the theory that he did not have too strong a propensity for vice.

Churchgoing was for him a kind of theatergoing, and the theater of that ingenuous New York, with its acrobats, dancers, clowns, and actors, was simply art. Play acting provided Henry with his first experience of economy and dash in form. He made himself sick from joy upon attending his first play, and never afterward lost the "sacred thrill" of the raising of the curtain. Playwriting was to be an obsession and a burden to him, while several of the novels are disguised plays. The smell of the theater never left him.

A glimpse of an actress of that day, Emily Mestayer, in her off-stage wrapper, gave him an early conception of the dark side of art: she was "a worn and weary, a battered even though almost sordidly smoothed, *thing* of the theater, very much as an old infinitely-handled and greasy violoncello of the orchestra might have been." He saw the used and hurt creator, the artist, as he would generalize later.

A few years later, Henry, misunderstanding the kind of artist that he was going to be, followed William, along with their friend, John La Farge, into William Hunt's studio at Newport, where he had otherwise spent his time reading the *Revue des Deux Mondes* and wishing that he were in Europe. He was quiet and happy in the studio, feeling, at seventeen, that here was art, full in the face. But he realized that his talent was limited to innocuous sketching when he saw what William could attempt, and he could not, in painting from life his cousin Gus Barker, posed gaily and handsomely, natural and naked, upon a pedestal.

He was strangling from a multitude of impressions and did not know what to do with them. He was too young and shy to admit that he lived for them and really on them. Only with the end of sketching he began to realize that he might possibly write, that, "even with canvas and brush whisked out of my grasp I still needn't feel disinherited."

In the form he had chosen, he had settled for his impressions and what he could make of them. The necessity for things composing rather than simply expressing stayed with him. Design, the structural or achitectonic sense: it is difficult to say whether his innate sense of this quality had caused him to attempt to draw or that drawing and studio life had taught it to him. It is essential in James. And in the large group of stories about artists, painting is as easy an illustration as writing of the primal curse and blessing of art.

Being seventeen years old, quivering in the new air of art, he had waked from heedless childhood into the meager atmosphere of an America in which he already felt an exile, without having gone away.

War came before he could make anything of his new situation. He was kept a civilian by a back injury, incurred in an attempt to put out a fire. At nineteen, in 1862, at Harvard, he lay flat a good part of the day, read law halfheartedly, watched the homesick soldiers drill on the college grounds, read letters from his brother Bob, who was fighting in the South, and mixed up the misery of his personal hurt with the melancholy of the public catastrophe. He wrote many years later in his memoirs:

One had the sense . . . of a huge comprehensive ache, and there were hours at which one could scarce have told whether it came most from one's own poor organism, still so young and so meant for better things, but which had suffered particular wrong, or from the enclosing social body, a body rent with a thousand wounds and that thus treated one to the honour of a sort of tragic fellowship.

It is certain that the injury hampered him throughout his life. He said as late as 1899 that he wrote literally *with* the back.

The suggestion has been made that James never married because the injury prevented his having a normal sexual life. And the inference is made that the fiction he wrote suffered from the author's enforced isolation from the full experience of living. The facts cannot, at this date, be ascertained. James left no direct evidence in the matter. A prosaic reason for his never marrying could as plainly be his obstinate idea that writing required the whole man. For a close reader, internal evidence carries more weight than unverifiable theory, and in the stories and novels the tone of his treatment of the sexual relations is normal. Or one might put it this way: the normal sexual relationship has the place of central and decisive importance in his fiction. One should remember this fact as one notes too the extremely wide and possibly morbid range of relationships possible among his creatures. It is the normal on which he builds. James was, after all, an earthbound writer, however subtle in method. There is no evidence in his books of a creator who had a hindered or a crippled appreciation of the passions— the normal passions. His fiction grows out of the passions. It feeds upon them as upon a source of vital good and vital evil.

What we can see as important in the situation in which he found himself as the Civil War began was the cruel fact that he found himself immobilized at a time when every one of his friends was going into the active, the public, the dramatic life. All of his morbid faculties were stimulated, all self-consciousness being understood in this sense as morbid. He was alone, he was different, he was hurt. Isolation and loneliness acted to force the luxuriant growth of the creative faculties.

Six years later, in 1869, when Henry James made his first adult trip to Europe, the one that decided his fate, he went, provisionally, as a semi-invalid. The joy that he felt in finding the new world of his imagination was accompanied by the fear of breaking down. However, there was nothing languid about his plunge into Europe. It was strenuous, an intoxication of the awakening powers of the imagination. The difference which "Europe" made (and James always considered Europe as a metaphor or symbol, a climate of the mind, as readily as he thought of it as a geographical entity) was that he found at last a society thick enough and complicated enough for the exercise of his social imagination. What was the despair of the sociologist was rich loot for the novelist. Nothing could be too bad. And it was the mixture of good and bad which his talents knew that they could use.

It is a serious misunderstanding of James to consider his flight from America to Europe as a confession of weakness, of a lack of stamina, of a confession of art-for-art's-sake attitude, or of general thinness. He went from the thin to the thick, from the comparatively simple toward the comparatively complex, into a rich culture where infinite possibilities in all possible forms attracted susceptible characters—thus he first saw his theme—the individual, representing the vital principle of life, entangled in a complex society, representing the forms which life might take.

James wrote a splendid lament for the American exile in *Roderick Hudson*:

It's a wretched business . . . this virtual quarrel of ours with our own country, this everlasting impatience that so many of us feel to get out of it. Can there be no battle then, and is one's only safety in flight? This is an American day, an American landscape, an American atmosphere. It certainly has its merits, and some day when I'm shivering with ague in classic Italy I shall accuse myself of having slighted them.

Within a few paragraphs of speaking these words, his hero, Roderick, goes gaily off to Europe, just as James himself snatched at the chance to take his American self into what his hero called an "immemorial, complex, accumulated" society. For James at this time already knew that he required the experience of objects which creaked and ground upon each other, peoples and institutions in conflict, habits, and beliefs which were the death one of the other.

James had found his place in going to Europe, but he did not become a European. He simply mixed explosive qualities, the American character and the European culture, and in the midst of the resultant conflicts picked out his material.

After trying Italy and France, he settled upon England as the best place to live and work. He suffered from his choice, particularly in the first years, when he was alone and unknown. But he had the cocky comfort of being ironical at the expense of the provincial national customs. He thought himself much lighter and altogether more cosmopolitan than the average Englishman. For company he walked the streets. He well knew their darkness and cruelty and poverty long before he knew any of the brilliant London interiors. The city's moral darkness struck him with horror; this darkness was an exhalation of ugliness, breathed out upon the beauty which lived upon it. "In

England," he wrote a friend in America, "the Huns and Vandals will have to come *up*—from the black depths of the (in the people) enormous misery."

None of these sterner perceptions were lost, although it might seem so when he was once fairly launched upon the glittering surface of London society. Success agreed with him, but success, coming as it did within a few years of his loneliness, simply enlarged his range. It gave him the full contrast of light and of dark.

For him, society, which he took to be his field, was the danger and wonder of people, people whose comparative money and leisure gave them the opportunity to get into trouble, to form relationships which would be subject to conflict, to be actors in the drama that only he might see. He was so constituted as the chameleon artist, in the sense Keats meant, that he must without choice live within the skin of everyone he met. As one novel succeeded another and he came to have the authority of a name, he became in his turn a performer in the London spectacle. He took part in the overt material drama with gusto. The submerged artist knew that the whole range of this world was, for his devious purposes, workable.

He wrote William later, in 1888, that at this most active period of his life he had had difficulty in finding time even to read in that social London

where, however, I took on board such an amount of human and social information that if the same necessary alternatives were presented to me again I should make the same choice. One can read when one is middle-aged or old; but one can mingle in the world with fresh perceptions only when one is young. The great thing is to be *saturated* with something—that is, in one way or another, with life; and I chose the form of my saturation.

The surface of his life continued to shine in the sun of London life, but, iceberg-like, the better part of that life was submerged in unremitting, bold work. He had had a late start, and each succeeding work after his first volume was a public *defi* of the powers of impotence. But an incomprehensible thing began to happen to him. He began to be an unread author.

This experience of waking to find himself unpopular came at a time when he could say soberly that he was writing better than he had ever written before, and that he was, as never before, bursting with ideas. To William Dean Howells, prosperous and popular in America, he wrote on the occasion of the New Year, 1888:

> I have entered upon evil days—but this is for your most private ear. It sounds portentous, but it only means that I am still staggering a good deal under the mysterious and (to me) inexplicable injury wrought—apparently—upon my situation by my two last novels, *The Bostonians* and *The Princess*, from which I expected so much and derived so little. They have reduced the desire, and the demand, for my productions to zero—as I judge from the fact that though I have for a good while past been writing a number of good short things, I remain irremediably unpublished. Editors keep them back, for months and years, as if they were ashamed of them, and I am condemned apparently to eternal silence.

The "good short things" for the year of the letter included the unsurpassable *The Lesson of the Master, The Liar,* and *The Aspern Papers.* In 1890 he brought out *The Tragic Muse,* and the next year, *The Pupil.* They left him and sent back no echo from the void. As an author, he was beginning to get a stone instead of bread; silence for work accomplished. The very reason for writing—communication—seemed to have failed. He had the strength to stand it. He found a place for his bitterness, adjusted his life to it, and worked away. He had the good workman's illogical faith in his work and added in his letter to Howells, "However, I don't despair for I think I am really in better form than I have ever been in my life, and I propose yet to do many things. Very likely too, some day, all my buried prose will kick off its various tombstones at once."

In the early 1890's he made his only conscious effort to escape his fate. He thought for a few years that he might make money and achieve the recognition for which he was starved by writing plays. He turned himself inside out in this, his "sawdust and orange-peel" phase, as he termed it. He wrestled with the form as with a devil or angel, and satisfied himself that he had put it in his pocket. One or two plays made a stir (there is an out-of-print edition of eight), but the public's amusement was mild. What he considered his best play, *Guy Domville,* failed sensationally. He wrote William in 1895:

Produce a play and you will know better than I can tell you, how such an ordeal—odious in its essence!—is made tolerable and palatable by great success; and in how many ways, accordingly, non-success may be tormenting and tragic, a bitterness of every hour, ramifying into every throb of one's consciousness. . . . I saw they couldn't care one straw for a damned young last-century English Catholic, who lived in an old-time Catholic world and acted, with every one else in the play, from remote and romantic Catholic motives.

It would be curious to see if *Guy* would play today.

Two years after the failure of *Guy Domville,* in 1897, James had accepted his fate, in almost a formal gesture, by leasing for twenty years a house of his own in the ancient city of Rye. He knew the act to be symbolic, a kind of settling himself down for the rest of his days to his own business. "I am just drawing a long breath from having signed—a few moments since—a most portentous parchment: the lease of a smallish, charming, cheap old house in the country. . . ." were his words to a friend.

Lamb House had proportion and the grace of having been lived in well. He reported to Howells that he was, "domiciled in some gentility, in a little old quasi-historic wainscotted house, with a real lawn and a real mulberry tree of my own to kick my heels on and under. . . ." The house had been in the residence of many past mayors of the old, shrunken walled city, whose glory, once considerable, had passed away. James was amused to speak of himself hereafter as "a small rude Sussex burgher."

He had at last found a burrow for himself, "a tight anchorage." Here he wrote book after book, and it was from here that he sent them into the world. It was a never finishing, always continuing life of writing, the unassuming, suave, and unnoted asceticism of the artist. A point should be made of the contradiction inherent in James' reputation as a social lion and the necessary self-denial of his actual work. His manner of living was austere and sacrificial even when it appeared to be social. He made no display of sacrifice. But Henry James as a social lion is a squint-eyed view of a complex man. He warmed to the social world, it fascinated him; he not only saw it as a show but saw into it, through it; it was the "fiery furnace" of people. He must have had wonderful manners, but he was no casual social lion. (A trick of his is ironic and poetic exaggeration of regret as a joke.) People in society, "the fiery furnace," were his material, his forces rubbing against each other, bending and breaking each other. He created, out of material pulled from this furnace, one "thing," one "artifex" after another. There is pathos in his gradual and finally irrevocable withdrawal after twenty-two years in London. Lamb House became a retreat where the "dingy" work went on.

Although the core of the life was work, the furnishings were pleasant. He made a garden; he refurnished the house. He opened the house to friends and relatives, particularly to the much loved children of his brother William. He varied his strict retirement by spring visits to London and annual vacations to the keener, Latin air of France or Italy.

It was only when, after years of living into Lamb House as into a second skin, upon considering a trip to America, his first in many, many years (he had last been there in 1882 and 1883), he knew for good how England had become the familiar and the known. Older, pushed by the fascination and difficulty of books to be done, it was awkward for him to dig himself out of his burrow for any great change. But he rose to his chance as to an adventure. It had the excitement of rediscovery; it was to be an expedition, this return to America.

In the fall of 1904 he set out. He was sixty-one, and the trip had become in his mind "the one chance that remains to me in life of anything that can be called a *movement:* my one ewe-lamb of possible exotic experience, such experience as may convert itself, through the sense, through observation, imagination and reflection now at their maturity, into vivid and solid *material,* into a general renovation of one's too monotinised grab-bag."

His subsequent rummage across the face of America in 1904 and 1905 was a sustained, rich vision of a land and a people seen without flattery and without denigration. He had the double sight of the native and the stranger. No travel book quite like the one he wrote upon his return to England can be found. He poured his sense of America into it, "such a living and breathing and feeling and moving great monster."

His trip to America was the climax of a period of calm and clarity, both physical and mental, a sense of well-being and poise that might well justify the long years in the country. In 1902 he had brought out *The Wings of the Dove,* in 1903, *The Ambassadors,* in 1904, *The Golden Bowl,* and in 1907, *The American Scene.*

But the trip was in fact almost the last fortunate occurrence in James' life. In 1910 William died, Henry reaching America again only to experience this miserable fact. His own health was bad. During several years that followed, he was able to write only in good moments snatched by force of will and desire out of the bad periods. Stories succeeded in getting done, but long things were more difficult. Two novels, *The Sense of the Past* and *The Ivory Tower,* both potentially greater than anything that had preceded them, remained fragments. And it was at this time that his publisher, Heinemann, advised him that he was destroying the plates of several of his unsellable novels.

In such precarious circumstances the loneliness of the country was more than he could bear. He began to live again more in London than in Rye:

I can no longer stand the solitude and confinement, the *immobilisation,* of that contracted corner in these shortening and darkening weeks and months. . . . [October, 1911] These things have the worst effect upon me—and I fled to London pavements, lamplights, shopfronts, taxi's—and friends; amid all of which I have recovered my equilibrium excellently, and shall do so still more.

He wrote the family book, as he called it, during these years, the memoirs of his father, his brother, just dead, his cousin Minnie Temple, and, as it turned out, the history of his own imagination, in *A Small Boy and Others, Notes of a Son and Brother,* and *The Middle Years,* the last left unfinished. The whole thing being, as any work done in those days, "a patch of ground wrested, from darkness and the devil!"

The unexpected disaster of the war broke upon him: "*This* was what we were so fondly working for!" He paid with his life at last for his imagination. The war simply engulfed him. Although his participation in it was through the nerves, it was complete and generous. He gave himself away in measuring his whole mind against it.

He began by believing that his English world had in a manner deserved the blow; that the war carried with it a kind of retribution, "the terrible sense that the people of this country may well —by some awful brutal justice—be going to get something bad for the exhibition that has gone on of their huge materialized stupidity and vulgarity." In the same breath came the thought, "almost the worst thing is that the dreadfulness, all of it, *may* become interesting. . . ." Here was the rub! He was seventy-one and frail, and yet he must in some way mix himself up with what was happening. The next step on his way into the absorption of all his interests in the great outward event was the thought of the people he lived among: "The stiffness and toughness of the country . . . the individualism which makes its force that of a collection of individuals and its voluntaryism of such a strong quality." Next: "Meanwhile I am myself of the most flaming British complexion."

James was like the ancient mulberry tree on his lawn at Lamb House which had recently been knocked over in a storm. On hearing of the event from a country neighbor, he wrote, "He might have gone on for some time, I think, in the absence of an *inordinate* gale—but once the fury of the tempest really descended he was bound to give way."

The World War was the inordinate gale which effectively descended upon the old man. However, he did not submit until he had committed to his letters the measurement of the artist's recording apparatus full length upon the life which swirled round him. He was infuriated that he was old, but he acted in so far as he could. He visited hospitals and raised money for them, he wrote pamphlets for Red Cross appeals. His application to become a British citizen represented no upheaval but a simple, stiff rectification of his position in the war. He believed in the British participation, and he had lived in England long enough to think that he should undo any falsity of appearance. He died shortly after he became a British citizen, and before he saw the end of the war.

Even essential facts may mislead. Those narrated above do not encompass the artist, but they show, at least, how his life provided a favorable background for his work. The minimum claim for the life is that it seems to have hindered him less than some other he might have led. One does not fancy him as a wage earner or as a money-maker.

He had the good fortune to be born in a family of intelligent human beings who encouraged freedom of the mind. His formal education was not rigorous: it passed over him, and he made his own way, imaginatively, as he grew up. He had no crippling inhibitions and no harmful reactions against youthful influences.

His tentative career in sketching prepared his eye for composition. Compose! Compose! was a constant watchword later. The pain of a youthful accident prepared him for the mental pain and isolation of the artist.

"Europe" simply brought him out, as it did many of his characters. The variety of scenes which he took in during his travels were settings he gathered in the armful. Money, a decent minimum, gave him all his life to write, and he was always decently grateful. The flourish of London success could only do him good. He had been such a vague, unassertive boy in America that finding his forms in what he might have termed, without commas, delightful old bad Europe, he found assurance and brilliance. He became a great talker as well as writer, and he wove for his friends webs of allusory fancy. You can catch that voice in the conversational tone of his plan for the uncompleted *The Sense of the Past,* which he dictated as it came, extemporaneously.

Any artist worth his salt can find difficulties and disappointments enough in his work to offset any amount of social comfort. The art becomes so absorbing that there is room for nothing else. So the artist, if he is Henry James, at last must exile himself from fascinating distractions, which he has, after all, mastered for his purposes. In retirement at Lamb House, he could call up at will the bright world, his "fiery furnace of people" who, reshaped now in tranquillity by their author-god, could find life again in the worlds of his stories.

The temptation that every artist suffers, to get out of his own life somehow, to escape the inhuman struggle with recalcitrant material, came to James in his bout of playwriting. He wrote ambiguously about his plays, seeming at times to respect the form and at others to be indulging in an unholy joy at escaping his fate. However, the effort failed, and, battered and sore, he withdrew again to Lamb House for "a little real writing."

There he remained until illness and war rudely interrupted.

But the facts do not define the man. The chameleon artist as well as the private individual escapes again. One cannot surprise James into any fixity of attitude except in relation to his work. He could enter any situation or any idea simply to get the feel of it from the inside. As he grew older and more sedentary in habit, his mind grew freer and bolder. He made new things out of old, as, for example, his great resolving of his old theme, the American in Europe, in its final form in *The Wings of the Dove, The Ambassadors,* and *The Golden Bowl,* old wine in new, symbolic bottles. His themes were pared down to utter simplicity while he struggled with more difficult uses of the themes. He had his excitement and his life, albeit of the inner kind.

Yet he was so freezingly alone in his work that as early as 1889 he could write to Robert Louis Stevenson in Samoa that he would send to his "dear Louis" his latest published work to read and comment upon, for "seriously and selfishly speaking I can't spiritually afford not to put the book under the eye of the sole and single Anglo-Saxon capable of perceiving—though he may care for little else in it—how well it is written." And he said in exhortation to Stevenson, and a little perhaps to himself, "Roast yourself, I beseech you, on the sharp spit of perfection, that you may give out your aromas and essences!"

James had no last-minute reprieve from neglect. He had to wait for posterity, as he predicted, to kick the tombstones off his collected works. What made him able to bear it was the trace of fanaticism in him, as in any "found" man. He knew what he was, and he had the courage to sit down and be himself. He had the morality of the artist which consists in knowing what one is about and then quietly getting to work with it.

As for appearances, which James always reveled in, he was an urbane, witty man, experienced, kind, hospitable, keen in seeing the relationships in things exposed and in those subterranean. He delighted in his house and in company in alternation to the stillness of his work hours. He had a polished brow, deep eyes, and a strong jaw. He was a slow but steady walker, a rounded, strolling figure, who rambled and talked. He was the most agreeable of men, but capable upon a point of being absolutely inflexible and pointedly true. He refused to join groups or make speeches or become a public literary figure. He liked to talk about writing and writers with the other craftsmen of his time who knew what they were doing, with Stevenson, Howells, A. C. Benson, Gosse, Kipling, Wells, and the youthful Hugh Walpole. Edith Wharton's automobile gave him in his last years an easier, freer kind of movement: he called it his "fleeing machine."

To say what he was not:

1. He was not Bohemian. His daring was mental, and even with its dash of diabolism, his exterior was simply modestly worldly. His friends reported a Buddhistic calm of authority behind the conservative, sedentary man's countenance.

2. He was not a man of a particular class, although he resembled, after the retirement to Rye, a country gentleman. Being an American, and in the bargain, a writer, he was agreeably statusless. But he thought all art conservative, in the literal, not political, meaning of the word.

3. He was not a democrat, but he was capable of getting inside the idea of radicalism. He admired his sister Alice's "passionate radicalism," and he created one of the most effective revolutionary figures in English literature, the enigmatic Paul Muniment, in *The Princess Casamassima.*

To try to say what he was: he was that "queer beast the artist," the alchemist who murmured to himself, "Convert, convert."

PART Two

Scope

"producing causes and produced creatures"

H ENRY JAMES' FIRST FEE FOR A PUBLISHED PIECE OF WRITING was $12. Charles Eliot Norton paid him that sum for a critical notice which appeared in *The North American Review.* He was twenty-one. The year was 1864. For several years thereafter, he continued to express himself with all the cocky confidence of youth in the pages of *The Nation, The Atlantic Monthly, The Galaxy,* and in Norton's magazine upon the subject of his elders, the great mid-century Victorians. The early notices are self-respecting but cursory, hypercritical, even patronizing. He is at his best on the novelists Dickens or Eliot, and at his worst on Walt Whitman. There are pieces collected from that period on Browning, Tennyson, Morris, Swinburne, Arnold, Ruskin, and Whistler. They remind one, when James seems primarily a twentieth century man, how very far back he went. He wrote at least 125 such notices within the ten-year period following the Civil War. He had, in a way, paid his respects to the older generation and squared his accounts with his predecessors by the time he began to think of himself as a writer.

The Story of a Year appeared in 1865, in the March issue of *The Atlantic Monthly;* it seems probable that this was James' first published story. In 1871 *Watch and Ward* came out as a serial in the same magazine. But this early novel had to wait seven years to make its appearance between book covers. In the meantime a volume of short stories, headed by the title story, *A Passionate Pilgrim,* was published in 1875. That year was also

19

the date of publication, in the *Atlantic Monthly,* of the author's first claimable novel, *Roderick Hudson.* With its appearance, the young man might consider himself launched as a published author. But he had waited. He was now thirty-two. He was under the burden of a lagging start, with the weight upon him of much to be said.

If 1864, the date of his first appearance in print, is taken as the beginning of his career as a writer, and the year 1916, the year of his death, as the end of that career, there is, in between, a long, long succession of months and years of constant production. It is a whole half century of writing. The statistics are impressive. The brute enumeration is as follows: novels, seventeen finished, two unfinished; stories, ninety-six counted and collected; memoirs, three volumes; travel sketches, volumes on England, France, America, and many scattered essays; biographies, two volumes; plays, six, at least, printed as plays, a number converted to story form; criticism, the great collection of the Prefaces, as well as several volumes of essays on novelists, poets, places, and ideas; letters, two volumes of general correspondence and several of particular.

For convenient reference there is listed below a selection of James' work. The novels are complete. The listing of the other works is an arbitrary selection designed to show the variety and fullness of his labor. The year cited is the date of book publication unless otherwise indicated.

	NOVELS	STORIES	OTHER
1865		The Story of a Year (in *The Atlantic Monthly*)	
1871	Watch and Ward (in *The Atlantic Monthly;* 1878, as book)		
1875	Roderick Hudson	A Passionate Pilgrim, Madame de Mauves (written in 1870 and 1873, respectively)	
1877	The American		
1878	The Europeans		French Poets and Novelists

	NOVELS	STORIES	OTHER
1879		Daisy Miller (in *The Cornhill Magazine* in 1878)	Hawthorne
1880	Confidence		
1881	Washington Square, Portrait of a Lady		
1883			Portraits of Places
1884			A Little Tour in France
1885		The Author of Beltraffio	
1886	The Bostonians, The Princess Casamassima		
1888		The Aspern Papers	Partial Portraits
1889		The Liar	
1890	The Tragic Muse		
1891		The Lesson of the Master, The Pupil, Brooksmith	
1893		The Middle Years	Essays in London and Elsewhere
1894			Theatricals: Two Comedies—Tenants and Disengaged
1895		The Coxon Fund, The Death of the Lion, The Next Time, The Altar of the Dead Glasses, The Figure in the	Theatricals: Second Series
1896	The Spoils of Poynton	Carpet	
1897	What Maisie Knew		
1898		In the Cage, The Turn of the Screw	
1899	The Awkward Age	"Europe"	
1900		The Great Good Place, Maud-Evelyn	
1901	The Sacred Fount		
1902	The Wings of the Dove		
1903	The Ambassadors	The Beast in the Jungle, The Birthplace	William Wetmore Story and His Friends

	NOVELS	STORIES	OTHER
1904	The Golden Bowl		
1905			English Hours
1907			The American Scene
1909		The Jolly Corner	Italian Hours
1910		The Bench of Desolation, The Velvet Glove	
1913			A Small Boy and Others
1914			Notes of a Son and Brother, Notes on Novelists
1915			England at War, Within the Rim and Other Essays (1914–15)
1917	The Ivory Tower,* The Sense of the Past *		The Middle Years *

* Published posthumously. James died on Feb. 28, 1916.

The author's wares are laid out for close survey and judgment. There was nothing abortive about his career. As a self-conscious artist, the only kind he respected, he stood behind them and assumed full responsibility. The following chapter is to be descriptive, rather than critical. An attempt will be made in it to show the size and shape of the world of which Henry James was creator and master. What he left out, what he put into his books should be ascertained first; then, afterward, one can walk into that world and try its values from the inside.

The range of experience which he knew and placed in his writings was narrow in one sense, but to this area of observation he had applied his imagination without reservation. The measurement of his understanding against his experience of life was a free one. James recognized no imposed limitations as to what he might or might not touch, and he rebuffed the idea of artificial boundaries.

He stated a belief in the artist's freedom of choice, explicitly in essay and implicitly in his novels. The following excerpt is from a critical work. In it he affirms: "The only obligation to which in advance we may hold a novel, without incurring the accusation of being arbitrary, is that it be interesting." James is commenting upon a pamphlet by Walter Besant, limiting the freedom of the artist in his choice of material, and continues:

He mentions a category of impossible things. . . . This seems to me to bring the novel back to the hapless little *rôle* of being an artificial, ingenious thing—bring it down from its large, free character of an immense and exquisite correspondence with life. . . . As Mr. Besant so justly intimates, it is all experience. That is sufficient answer to those who maintain that it must not touch the sad things of life, who stick into its divine unconscious bosom little prohibitory inscriptions on the end of sticks, such as we see in public gardens—"It is forbidden to walk on the grass; it is forbidden to touch the flowers; it is not allowed to introduce dogs or to remain after dark; it is requested to keep to the right." The young aspirant in the line of fiction whom we continue to imagine will do nothing without taste, for in that case his freedom would be of little use to him but the first advantage of his taste will be to reveal to him the absurdity of the little sticks and tickets.

From a novel, *The Tragic Muse*, comes an affirmation in the indirect form James loved, a statement by a character in the novel. It is an old actress speaking. She has been reproached for playing, always, "bad women," and her answer shows the difficulty as well as the necessity of being true:

To be too respectable to go where things are done best is in my opinion to be very vicious indeed; and to do them badly in order to preserve your virtue is to fall into a grossness more shocking than any other. To do them well is virtue enough, and not to make a mess of it the only respectability. That's hard enough to merit Paradise. Everything else is base humbug!

For the reflecting mind must be true to itself. The type of mind at work is the reflecting one; the function of that mind is to compose; the source material for that reflecting mind is the human and social scene.

To block in the area of James' natural territory, it is first helpful to explore its boundaries and see what lies beyond them. It is obvious that there are vast tracts of human experience on which James never set foot. Yet one is not so much aware of this while reading him, for he is a skillful persuader.

He carries the reader into worlds of which that person has, in most cases, only a hearsay knowledge, and perhaps in his own living, very little sympathy. The author, in effect, asks first for a suspension of prejudice. Then, upon presentation of the ele-

ments of his story, a circle of references which contains all the
principles necessary for understanding the characters as they
move within that circle; the author asks for a transfer of sympathy to this made world which is for a time to occupy the reader.

Having given his attention and his sympathy, the trick is
worked, and the reader has got himself inside the framework
which James has erected. As long as the spell lasts, he is thinking
the thoughts of the characters and feeling their emotions. He
understands what Roderick Hudson and Isabel Archer want out
of Europe, or what Christina Light wants out of Roderick, or
Gilbert Osmond out of Isabel. It is like a game. Once everyone
has agreed to pretend—and James has an easy grace in asking the
favor—the rest comes easily. Bold verisimilitude convinces of the
reality of these worlds while the hanging suspense of what is to
happen next takes care of the reader's keeping up, after he has
once been caught.

The innocent, impatient reader has slipped into the Jamesian
world where there are new suns and new moons. But he believes
in them, likes their shining, and may even, for the time come to
be impatient of any other light in the sky. He espouses—for
understanding, for amusement, for whatever he calls his enjoyment of fiction—the world of the author. He forgets there is any
other kind of world. He stares amazed upon awaking to see the
various kinds of living of which James takes no account.

First of all, there is the great gap of the space occupied by the
natural as an active agent in man's life. Nature (aside from
human nature) is not a force in James. It is a setting. His characters do not cope with the elements of rain, snow, heat, or cold
in any dynamic relationship. He was, remember, "very towny
and domesticated." He lost a whole field of reference, in consequence, but he had a familiar acquaintance with the domesticated landscape, in which the land and the human figure, with
all its works, comfortably mingled.

He was even more apt to wring a sort of pathos out of the
smudged turf of a big city park where nature was sorely pushed
to assert itself at all. Two scenes effective in their juxtaposition
of the private emotion with the shabby public scene are those of
Verena's and Ransom's close passage by the shores of love in Central Park in *The Bostonians* and Milly's long, staring leave-

taking of life in her afternoon spent on a bench in Regent's Park in *The Wings of the Dove.*

He was sensitive to air and light as an appropriate bath of atmosphere for his characters. He often referred to a description of the weather the weight of emotion oppressing his heroes: such a transfer is effected in the scene of the storm near the end of *The Spoils of Poynton* and in the scene of another storm lashing Milly's palace on a Venetian canal in *The Wings of the Dove*. In *The Ambassadors* the air of Paris, rather than logic, takes hold of Strether and diverts him from sensible and explicable purposes. James thus uses an old device in extending the inner life into the atmosphere of the day, whether congenial or inimical, but he uses it sparingly and effectively. In moments of climax, he lifts the story into the widest, most allusive beauty. He conveys more than the bare story should be able, on its own, to do.

A few lines from *The Sacred Fount* follow. The narrator is describing the parklike forest through which he is walking, where in a few minutes he is to meet May Server, the tragic, misused heroine of the story: "There was a general shade in all the lower reaches—a fine clear dusk in garden and grove, a thin suffusion of twilight out of which the greater things, the high tree-tops and pinnacles, the long crests of motionless wood and chimnied roof, rose into golden air. The last calls of birds sounded extraordinarily loud; they were like the timed, serious splashes, in wide, still water, of divers not expecting to rise again." Coming through the trees, he sees the figure of the woman approaching him: "It was exactly as if she had been there by the operation of my intelligence, or even by that—in a still happier way—of my feeling."

James generally preferred subdued weather, an effect as if nature were conforming to the human creature's emotional needs. In *Madame de Mauves,* Longmore, fallen back in dejection from a baffling encounter with Euphemia de Mauves, finds that the landscape itself bears in its negativeness the marks of the grayness and coolness which he had discerned in her denial of passion: "The fields and trees were of a cool metallic green; the grass looked as if it might stain your trousers; and the foliage your hands. The clear light had a sort of mild grayness; the sunbeams were of silver rather than gold."

Nature as an elemental force or as a stubborn thing to be lived with, a not entirely adaptable power, does not exist. Even the "bristling primeval glacier" in the Switzerland of the story *The Private Life* exists as a piquant backdrop for conversation which might as well have taken place in London, in one of his drawing rooms whose note of nature would be a row of flowerpots upon a window ledge giving upon a dusty square.

It is the outsider's viewpoint of the natural that he showed, the cultivated man's projection of his moods into the lines of land and sea, or the artist's perception of design in the light and shade of meadow and hedgerow, wood and spire. There is no word for the man who works with the unconscious elements, who lives off them or is destroyed by them; nothing of the fisherman, the sailor, the farmer, the woodsman; nothing of the frontier, which, as he wrote, was occupying so much of the energy of his native land; nothing of the brute force of nature which could work so upon a people to shape or break them.

If one sets aside the primitive as beyond James' interest, there is left the entire social field. But broad areas of organized living were also over his horizon. Its big public noises—war, revolution, electoral struggles, reform movements, nationalism—were mostly so. However, in a manner which emphasizes their peripheral interest for him, he treated, at least once, each one of these big public noises.

War, which James never experienced personally, although he saw his wounded brother brought home on a stretcher during the Civil War, is only an echo in the early stories and novels. But war, remembered darkly by Christopher Newman, "the American," seems to have been one of the reasons for that person's stiff about-face in his manner of living, a turnabout from brutal, exciting money-making, to, first, a dead stop for painful breathing, and then a look about to see what else life held besides fighting a war and getting money. You get a gasp of disgust from an expert practitioner of two kinds of fighting, the military and the civil, when Newman pulls up in mid-career, in the Grantian era after the Civil War, and literally stops his cab driver, on the way to making a deal in Wall Street, in order to set out, at that split second, in a deliberately opposite direction.

Revolution, which James, while savoring the amenities of the cushioned classes, never lost sight of as that group's possible end, fills one novel from cover to cover: *The Princess Casamassima*. It is simply the story of a revolution, a revolution forever waited, forever coming, an outbreak of public violence whose occurrence will mean the literal end of the hero. For Hyacinth Robinson, the bookbinder, the bastard of a prostitute, as he harshly names himself, has given his life into the hands of a group of plotters. An act of violence, probably a political assassination, which he has sworn to perform when called upon, hangs over him from the beginning of his story to the end.

While James had taken a specific terroristic act as the most dramatic and workable example of the revolutionary spirit available, he showed an understanding of the whole social milieu which would tend to cause such an act to take place. This novel has as a pervading odor the trouble of the poor. And as a disruptive force, he exhibited an intelligence planted in the mind of an artisan of this black London, a worker who had a personal grudge against society.

Next he showed the plotters, the usual, talkative, discontented group of superior workers into which Hyacinth had wandered; they wanted a change, but they did not know how to bring it about. They were all too loose, too vague, too doctrinaire, too amateurish to cause an explosion.

Then he introduced into that group Paul Muniment, who is all will, the model of the selfless revolutionist, perhaps of the Communist worker before such a person existed. Paul is as gifted, as ruthless, and as cool as a revolutionist should be, and he leaves wasteful enthusiasm to others who become his tools. In his stained chemist's apron Paul Muniment convinces his fellow conspirators, who do not like him, and also James' reader, that he will some day be a prime minister.

Into the equally ferocious but less violent civil contests, those of electioneering and politicking, James threw as likely a young hero as Hyacinth. Nick Dormer, whose story is only the third strand of *The Tragic Muse*, is a flattered young man of good family and prepossessing appearance who is pushed by a political family and an ambitious fiancée into standing for Parliament. The chapters which describe the manner in which Julia Dallow, Nick's forceful and beautiful friend, manipulates the election and, in effect, gives him her district, is an amusing lesson in cynical politics. As he had shown an understanding of the forces leading to bloodshed in public life, James showed here an understanding of the powers which merely bend the public will to their way rather than break it.

Bostonian reform, in the novel *The Bostonians,* is another area of public effort which James essayed in one classic example. He showed again competent understanding of a world generally thought outside his range. There has seldom been a better picture of the women's rights movement, its advocates and opponents, than in this novel: the tone is both satirical and romantic, an interesting and fertile mixture. He encompassed the two poles, Olive Chancellor, the tragic, narrow reformer, and Basil Ransom, the engaging, unrepentant reactionary. That Verena, who is neither essentially advocate nor opponent, is the center of the story, rather gives away the secret: that James was writing not about reform, but about Olive and Ransom and Verena.

He tackled the modern shibboleth of nationalism in a story, *Collaboration,* in which a French poet and a German composer, just after the close of the Franco-Prussian War, lose the regard of friends and family in order to write together an opera which they cannot do separately.

It is beside the point to say in the light of these examples that James could, if he would. If these stories are outside his main line of interest, they are not freaks. For all their revolution and reform, examined closely, they disclose that the subject in each case is not, squarely, war, revolution, reform, or nationalistic prejudice. The subject is the development of the person involved in the struggle.

In the first case, that of *The American,* revulsion against war merely sends Newman into the private life with a vengeance. He bends his stiff, dry, Western will to encompass pictures, sculpture, the French royalist society, and the means of extracting a wife from a jealous family.

In the second case, *The Princess Casamassima,* the center of attention is not so much the outcome of the revolution as the outcome of the struggle within Hyacinth which seems destined to split him in two. He has not only the distinction of being a key tool of the coming revolution, he is also a mind and a soul. In the waiting period he has become involved in a dilemma as to the relative value of blasting or preserving the better results of civilization.

In *The Tragic Muse* the brilliant rendering of the electoral scene at Julia's country seat, Harsh, is actually to one side of the main line of Nick's development. The fact that Nick, as a complicated young man, could become bored at public success and desire instead the private career of a portrait painter constitutes the real center of his story.

James was a camp follower of ideas. He could use any one that he could understand. And comprehension did not in his case mean being for or against the idea. The idea, whether political, economic, or religious, was an element in his characters' lives, not his. It is really irrelevant to the success of the story to find out whether the author believed or did not believe in revolution or reform. It may be interesting, aside from criticism, to ferret out his private sympathies, but it is not necessary. The novels and the tales contain their own points of reference.

Money is of tremendous importance as a condition of life, a condition for freedom, for mischief-making, for the cultivation of eccentricity, for egotism, in all James' stories. It is also the crux of struggles between characters who want to inherit it, to marry it, to give it away for a price, or to avoid it in order not to pay a price. But the ways of getting money, the two opposite ends of the scale, wage earning and profit making, are seldom seen as activities which his characters perform before the eye of the reader.

The exceptions prove the case. For the wage earners, there are several governesses, a number of journalists, one rising diplomat, an assortment of minor government officials, one doctor, one bookbinder, one chemist, one shopgirl, one telegraph clerk, and innumerable daubers and scribblers, among whom are hack, genius, and industrious mediocrity. Outside this handful it is hard to recall any others of James' people who have not fortunately got the means to live without the daily grubbing effort.

The government officials assemble for the great part in Mrs. Brook's drawing room in *The Awkward Age:* they speak in an off-hand manner of this or that one's good position—"rivers and lakes, you know." But the only function one sees them perform is the dexterous trafficking in one another's personal affairs. The potential ambassador is Peter Sherringham in *The Tragic Muse*. But one sees him, not at work, but in his customary seat at the Comédie-Française or in Miriam Rooth's dressing room. The doctor, the strong-minded freethinker of *Washington Square*, may at some hour go diligently upon his rounds, but the reader sees him only in the act of meddling in his daughter's happiness.

Governesses are a more portentous business. A very early, colorless one narrates the story *Master Eustace,* and a timid, proper one in *A London Life* is frightened by her master's drunkenness. But governesses, if not in life, at least in English fiction, are touchstones for the odd, the ominous, or the improper. James does not neglect so good a tradition. The young governess in *What Maisie Knew* is improper and gay even if she does become Papa's wife. The young lady in *The Turn of the Screw* is, after Jane Eyre, the English governess who has the most to contend with in imperious young masters and mysterious old houses. The nurse, the good, ugly, kind woman in *Maisie,* is far from being a background fixture; she is a determining force in the outcome of the story.

Journalists excited James' wrath and amusement. The one in *The Reverberator,* a gossip columnist of his day, spoils Francie Dosson's chances of marrying well in Paris. The magazine editor, Beston, in *John Delavoy,* is censorious and Philistine. Howard Bight in *The Papers* assumes some dignity only by the magnitude of his crime, the pushing of a public figure (as he thinks) to ruin and suicide by industrious publicity. The heroes of *The Wings of the Dove* and *The Ambassadors* are journalists, but the newspaper and magazine world of their background is dim. It is in the short stories mentioned above rather than in the novels that James reported the workaday world of the press. The light and excitement of the streets where the noisy, senseless headline is shouted; the cramped, greasy eating place of the reporters; the cynical atmosphere of the Fleet Street editor's office: all are detailed with gusto.

The work scenes of the dark side of *The Princess Casamassima* and of the story *In the Cage* are, however, the only ones to be examined soberly, or rather imagined, by the author as day-long, year-long places of confinement where one must go and stay and conform in order to live. The title of the second one describes its prisonlike quality. Its heroine is a counter girl for a neighborhood telegraph and postage office. The fact that the cramped office, with a grocer sharing the quarters, is in a Mayfair street dangles before the girl the idea of another kind of life. It emphasizes the fact of her confinement "in the cage." Hyacinth's bookbindery in *The Princess Casamassima,* where he wears an apron and works at a bench, is his one place of repose in the novel. His liking for the work allies him with the artists in James' catalogue.

James was at home among the writers, painters, sculptors, and actors of so many of his tales. Whatever else he was, his artist was a worker. The author included in his list every type from hack to genius. The devoted mother of *Greville Fane* is a hack; she supports pretentious children by wearisome, fluent ink-stained effort. On the other hand, Ray Limbert in *The Next Time* is a genius who wants to write something that will be popular and help feed his family, who cannot eat his critical reputation. But try as he will, he can only turn out one fine, unpopular book after another. The family problem remains unsolved.

James had a curiosity about every phase of a writer's life, about his relations to society as well as to his work, about his selling rate as well as his inspiration. He presented samples of every degree of attention to work, from the trifler, Leolin, in *Greville Fane,* to the compromised master, St. George, in *The Lesson of the Master,* who shut himself into a grim, dark room to write standing up to a waist-high bookkeeper's desk to the end that his wife might be dressed and entertained as she wished.

In his own experience James had learned that the writer does not fit into society as a necessary cog. The artist is always a special case. He must make his own place and please himself if possible; have, as James said of himself, "a general plan and a private religion." The fun was to see how different temperaments adjusted themselves; how some beat the game and how others were beaten by it. James made his reader see the struggle, now comically, now tragically.

As for the process of money or profit making, it was as mysterious to him as a hidden social ritual to which he had never gained admittance. It was what all America did, all except the Jameses, with tireless energy and effort. The mark of it was upon the retired millionaires he saw crossing his path in Europe.

But the effect of wealth is all-important. Money in *The Portrait of a Lady* gives Isabel Archer her chance to look around; in *The Ambassadors* money from the manufacture of some household utensil sends Strether to Europe. Her father's money floats Maggie Verver in *The Golden Bowl* into marriage with her ungrateful Prince. Money, the dead, scattered family's money, gives the orphaned Milly Theale in *The Wings of the Dove* her last fling at life. Money is important. However, in not one of these cases is the clever hand which made the money shown turning the trick.

What James did was to do what he could. He showed the results which were observable. His particular interest was in the rich man converted, the Christopher Newman, the Adam Verver, who has had a second chance, who has set aside money-making for life, or what James called life. These men are types of force or will who have become doubly formidable by the addition of sensibility.

James had a nature which was aware of the most delicate of moral shades. In his tales he built action and counteraction upon the effective weight of moral qualities. Yet he was indifferent to a theological explanation of life.

He had discovered certain constant elements in human nature, and he reported these causes and effects as he observed them. He had perhaps the religious sensibility without the resource of a religious theory. Nowhere in him will one find a meaning from which one could infer a belief in the supernatural, or in one final, irrefutable explanation of the human plight. (There is one important exception to this statement which will be touched upon later, but its isolation only emphasizes the general absence of religious speculation upon the part of the novelist.)

Yet James' picture of life is in essential agreement with that of those who go beyond him to resolve the enigma of good and evil at some point in eternity. He does not resolve; he does not reconcile. But the agony and the evil are there, squarely before one.

James came as near to a statement of philosophy as he was capable of doing (as one could who saw meaning always in objective appearances and never abstracted from them) in a letter to his friend Grace Norton upon the occasion of a death in her family in 1883:

I am determined not to speak to you except with the voice of stoicism. I don't know *why* we live—the gift of life comes to us from I don't know what source or for what purpose; but I believe we can go on living for the reason that (always of course up to a certain point) life is the most valuable thing we know anything about, and it is therefore presumptively a great mistake to surrender it while there is any yet left in the cup. In other words consciousness is an illimitable power, and though at times it may seem to be all consciousness of misery, yet in the way it propagates itself from wave to wave, so that we never cease to feel, and though at moments we appear to, try to, pray to, there is something in the universe which it is probably good not to forsake. You are right in your consciousness that we are all echoes and reverberations of the *same*, and you are noble when your interest and pity as to everything that surrounds you, appears to have a sustaining and harmonizing power. Only don't I beseech you *generalize* too much in these sympathies and tendernesses—remember that every life is a special problem which is not yours but another's, and content yourself with the terrible algebra of your own. Don't melt too much into the universe, but be as solid and dense and fixed as you can. . . . Sorrow comes in great waves—no one can know that better than you—but it rolls over us, and though it may almost smother us it leaves us on the spot, and we know that if it is strong we are stronger, inasmuch as it passes and we remain. It wears us, but we wear it and use it in return; and it is blind, whereas we after a manner see.

His stories bear out this thought. They exhibit a tension between the conscious individual and the raw material of life. That person has two duties in living: the first, to expose himself to as much of the great unconscious force of life as he is able to endure; the second, to hold firm to that irreducible core which is himself, to be what and who he is with all his might. Upon the one hand, there is the assault of the multiplied battery of life; and upon the other, the integrity of the individual; the link between the two being the necessary tension of the personal consciousness. If there is more, James will not gainsay it;

but neither is he able to affirm it except gropingly and tentatively.

Here are rather lightly worded confessions, excerpts torn from several letters to various friends over a long period of his life. They are mutilated fragments but will serve as well, since he did not hold with system or theory. They illustrate the vivacity and spirit of his unbelief.

In 1898 Henry read his brother's lecture on "Immortality," in which William had classified man as either a "yearner" or an "objector" to the idea of the life after death. He had admired "the art and interest in it," he wrote his sister-in-law Alice; but he put William on notice that he refused to be categorized: "I am afraid I don't very consciously come into either of the classes it is designed to pacify—either that of the yearners, I mean, or that of the objectors. It isn't the difficulties that keep me from yearning—it is somehow the lack of the principle of the same."

Another word of his is significant, this excerpt from another letter to Grace Norton:—"though I don't pray, in general, and don't understand it." Two lines from letters to A. C. Benson in 1896 follow: "I have the imagination of disaster—and see life indeed as ferocious and sinister." And: "I am afraid I am not quite the creature of abysmal calm that you appear to glance at. However, let me not blaspheme against the jealous gods—before whom I make it a law to wriggle constantly on my stomach."

It is remarkable that he kept his gaiety and flexibility, which were as sincere as his melancholy. He wrote to W. E. Norris in 1904, when he was already sixty-one, this youthful pronouncement: "Save at frequent moments when I desire to die very *soon*, almost immediately, I cling to life and propose to make it last. I blush for the frivolity, but there are still so many things I want to do."

Even in 1914, with his brother William already dead, and dead in such a way as to give Henry "the ultimate ache," with his own health ruined, he could yet rebuke Henry Adams for a systematic despair. His own despair had always been chancy and haphazard. The passage is long but very characteristic:

I have your melancholy outpouring of the 7th and I know not how better to acknowledge it than by the full recognition of its unmitigated blackness. *Of course* we are lone survivors, of course the past that was our lives is at the bottom of an abyss—if the abyss *has* any bottom; of course, too, there's no use talking unless one particularly *wants* to. But the purpose, almost, of my printed divagations was to show you that one *can*, strange to say, still want to—or at least behave as if one did. I still find my consciousness interesting—under *cultivation* of interest. Cultivate it *with* me, dear Henry—that's what I hoped to make you do—to cultivate yours for all that it has in common with mine. *Why* mine yields an interest I don't know that I can tell you, but I don't challenge or quarrel with it—I encourage it with a ghastly grin. You see I still, in presence of life (or what you deny to be such) have reactions—as many as possible—and the book I sent you is a proof of them. It's, I suppose, because I am that queer monster, the artist, an obstinate finality, an inexhaustible sensibility.

It was the continued curiosity about the inexhaustibility of consciousness that at last led him into speculations about immortality. His way of envisioning immortality was just in the limitless spread of consciousness. The idea, expressed only late in life, was not so much a contradiction of earlier ideas as a stretching and extension of them.

What saved him—from intellectual sterility and pride, from despair, and from a mental old age—also killed him. He could never lose his ability to take in. Even the war came to that: a killing interest. "Almost the worst thing is that the dreadfulness, all of it, *may* become interesting," he wrote on July 31, 1914, to Sir Claude Phillips. Good or bad as his circumstances might be; whether they lifted him buoyantly or turned to smash him, he held yet to a profane interest in them.

In his stories he did what he could with the usages of organized religion. The observation of religious forms is fairly frequent, although it is significant that it is the secondary, not the primary, characters who go through the forms. (Maggie Verver is a Roman Catholic, but not in any vital reference.) However, when the forms were appropriate, he made use of them, but generally assigned them to the lesser characters, to the exotic, the foreign, and the alien persons.

He never showed the inside of the mind of the practitioner. When Christina Light wept at the foot of the altar, when Madame de Mauves became a Carmelite nun, James was showing appropriate reactions, given the personality and the background of the performer. The forms of the Roman Catholic Church, being the most outside his own nature, the most exotic to his experience, and the most grateful to his sense of style, received at his hands the most dignity of presentation. As much as he admired these forms, it must be understood that it was a purely objective and imaginative admiration, that of the artist using the modes of worship as he did the other forms which society had devised, in order to exhibit and represent that society in all its fullness.

He was helpless with the loose and varied ecclesiastical forms of his own country. He had known no parsons in his youth. He had to invent them when they were necessary for his stories. They might be human, but they were not of the cloth. His clergyman in the first novel, *Watch and Ward,* is the most worldly of the characters in the book. The theological student in the story *A Light Man* has only a certain hangdog modesty as the badge of his profession; his activities are as cynical as those of the "light man" of the title.

Religious observation in the English stories is almost entirely a matter of picture, a familiar one being the pretty walk from manor to village church, repeated again and again in the stories of the country week end. Churchgoing appears as neither more nor less than a part of the prescribed social activity, a part of the week-end ritual of tea on the lawn, dinner in the state dining room, withdrawal of the ladies with candles upstairs, and of the gentlemen to the smoking room.

Criticism of religion in James is criticism of its social aspects. He showed in his treatment of little Aggie in *The Awkward Age* and of Pansy Osmond in *The Portrait of a Lady* that he did not consider convent education the best training for a young girl who, upon leaving the convent, would be thrown into the corruption of society. He showed, too, in his picture of Madame de Cintré's withdrawal into a convent in *The American* that he thought such a withdrawal a perversion of life. However, he did show that her self-immolation in this particular manner was her only means of self-assertion or of independent action. The Catholicism of her family was only one strand of its character, other important strands being its royalism, its cult of family; all the strands together were needed to comprehend the De Cintrés' thoughts and actions, among which were the daughter's with-drawal into a convent and the son's death in a duel.

There is no questioning of the sincerity of such actions, per-verted as they might seem to the comparatively straight, simple American, Newman. They were actions which educated him. They made him see that life was made up of many sincerities, of many kinds of sincerities, and that some were the death of others. A contradiction, a strange, minor theme throughout James, is an irregular but strong tendency to self-denial, to self-sacrifice, akin to, but without reference to, a religious motive. Characteristic examples are Isabel's return to Osmond at the end of *The Portrait of a Lady* and Fleda Vetch's strained and over-refined denial of her instincts in *The Spoils of Poynton*.

The introduction of the ghostly element may at first sight seem a contradiction. But the most worldly of authors was to find that the supernatural was best handled in cold blood. Such tales as *The Turn of the Screw, Maud-Evelyn, The Private Life, The Jolly Corner,* and *The Sense of the Past,* all have their systems of belief wrapped up inside the narrative. None of them point to a revelation outside the story.

Consideration of the mentality of the James hero shows how little place religion proper has in his novels. None of them are of a mystical temperament. Isabel Archer, Hyacinth Robinson, Verena Tarrant, Miriam Rooth, Maisie Farrange, Lambert Strether, or Milly Theale: all are skeptics by temperament. Each one is his own authority, his own touchstone; a character-istic so marked as to amount to a profane Protestantism. Some of them are managed, more or less, by other, stronger characters; their absolution, coming from their creator-author, occurs only when they recognize their own responsibility of choice. The highest degree of drama in James comes at this moment of sharp-est, most tragic insight, when Hyacinth or Isabel or Lambert Strether recognizes what he is and what he has done. The load upon the human heart is almost unbearable, since there is no relief in prayer or any kind of abdication of the imagination or understanding.

A thoughtful study of his novels only raises another ques-tion. If James was not answered by conventional, organized re-ligion, what served the man? He was not a determinist. His creatures are positive forces in the world; they are not entirely made by it. One is left with the mysterious relationship which he demonstrates, the interdependence of the individual and the world. He will not, or cannot, explain what constitutes the integrity of the individual (even when defeated), nor how this peculiar quality came to be within the person. But he does demonstrate that such an inexplicable element lives and in some manner (as he had shaped his stories) works in the raw material of life to shape an existence which has the distinction of form.

The preceding discussion has only gone around the circle, the outer edge of James' world. It remains to fill it in, to color it, to people that world, to show its sources in his field of observation. It was an incisive art which made so narrow a field serve to mean so much. For it was a small, bright world that he owned. It floated somehow in its floodlight on top of the dark mass of energy and effort, of the dark forces, social, political, and religious, necessary to set free the few who could afford the luxury of personal relations.

James was a man who could see organized society as it was in its richness of good and evil and see it steadily, without the necessity of an invidious theory. He did not wish it changed or smashed. It was a good stage for his people, who were the luxury products of the age. In a way they are the equivalent of the kings of classical and Renaissance drama. They live exempt from the common hobbles, freed for larger fates. Leisure, freedom of movement, exemption from day labor, all throw the Jamesian hero into the exceptional mold. It is only in the air of dangerous freedom that the specifically human and social emotions develop.

Here they assume size, shape, and force. The distinctive, typical human trait has a luxurious growth. Since it is the typical human trait, his hero represents mankind. Even in his atypical situation at the top of the heap, he is a genuine man. Therefore, although he worked a narrow field, the fragile, mannered one of "society," James cut deep. His people are real people. It is simply by the artificiality of their world, by the barrier set up between them and the common economic struggle, that the basic human traits gain scope. The fact is that James underlined this theme even more deliberately. He contrasted always the natural, spontaneous human creature, the naïve child, the innocent young girl, the rusticated old man, the unequipped New World person, each one, with the made, artificial world into which his story takes him.

For the purpose of the immediate point—James' scope—his equation of the individual plus society equaling story may simply be stated and not elaborated. Its central meaning in the total work will be more evident later.

Given the man that James was, with no knowledge or interest in the primitive or in the natural, with no desire to explain mankind by the special pleading of a religious, economic, or political theory, there is left for consideration his proper world, that of personal and social relationships in a highly organized civilization. The fact that he was the last great novelist of the twentieth century who could assume a stable society is an important fact. For whether his characters are masters or victims of this civilization of which they are the most conspicuous members, the enfolding organization is assuredly a fact. These characters may fight it, conquer it, or be thrown to die on its sharp edges; yet it remains an incontrovertible, stony-hearted fact.

Since his time the novelist has had to assume the opposite condition, that is, the collapse of society. The sensation has been that of slipping foundations and crumbling walls. The storytellers who are his heirs suffer from this; by putting all significance into the exaggerated sensibility of a principal character and then allowing that sensibility to exercise its perceptions in a void, their stories have a faintness that his do not.

James in his own life was certain that his world was collapsible. He thought it top-heavy, rotten, and materialistic. He even foretold its end in violence. Yet while he lived, it could not be got round, it must be faced.

Yet in facing it, he was not the grim moralist whose first purpose in seeing was to do. James' impulse upon perceiving was to see yet more and more, to understand, to comprehend, and then to translate that understanding into a series of stories which would contain in special forms the equivalent pressure of the initial perception. His first morality was that of the artist, and he knew that for art's ulterior purposes, evil was as necessary as good. In sober sense he might deplore the congested upper

classes, the restricted poor; yet the spectacle of London life re-
sulting from the differentiation of class was a picture of dazzling
appropriateness for his pen.

Rather than deplore, he simply enjoyed, with the special,
transforming enjoyment of the artist. On the subject of empire,
as seen from its nerve center, London, he wrote home to Grace
Norton in 1885 (the year of Gordon's death at Khartoum):

I find such a situation as this extremely interesting and it makes
me feel how much I am attached to this country and, on the whole,
to its sometimes exasperating people. The possible *malheurs*—re-
verses, dangers, embarrassments, the "decline," in a word, of old
England, go to my heart, and I can imagine no spectacle more touching, more thrilling and even dramatic, than to see this great precarious, artificial empire, on behalf of which, nevertheless, so much of
the strongest and finest stuff of the greatest race (for such they are)
has been expended, struggling with forces which perhaps, in the long
run, will prove too many for it. If she only will struggle, and not collapse and surrender and give up a part which, looking at Europe as
it is to-day, still may be great, the drama will be well worth watching
from (such) a good, near standpoint as I have here.

James' attitude to what he put in the novels and tales was
the same. What counted was essential drama. And he was so
constituted that drama appealed to him in specific forms. He
thought in and through representation. He understood later
that it was his father's abstracting faculty of thought that had
caused him as a boy to feel a wordless sense of irritation and uneasiness at "Father's Ideas." "I gaped imaginatively, as it were,
to such a different set of relations," and had "need of those objective appearances that my faculty seemed alone fitted to grasp."
The dreary weight of old civilizations failed to depress him.

He argued the matter thus with W. D. Howells: "I sympa-
thize even less with your protest against the idea that it takes an
old civilisation to set a novelist in motion—a proposition that
seems to me so true as to be a truism. It is on manners, customs,
usages, habits, forms, upon all these things matured and established, that a novelist lives—they are the very stuff his work is
made of." He put his preferences more lightly to William
Roughead, of the Juridical Society of Edinburgh, who had been
sending him from time to time some of the literature of crime,

including the records of the witchcraft trials of the time of James I: "Do, very generously, send me the sequel to your present study—my appetite has opened to it too; but then go back to the dear old human and sociable murders and adulteries and forgeries in which we are so agreeably at home."

Appearances, now revealing, now hiding, but always related to the significant inner reality: these were his natural preoccupations. To such a nature even clothes could be important. The very ribbons and ruffles upon the exquisitely ignorant Daisy Miller were a sign. Idea lived in dress, in manner, in gesture, in action. Truth had a local habitation or none at all for him.

James was lucky in his time. This period of peace between wars allowed all the civilian vices and virtues space for strange growths. His people, like their creator, were given to a free and easy moving about across the map. They had a freedom which we, in our cramped quarters, with ten times the facility for speed, so grievously lack. The germ of a story would come to him with background complete and easily varied: rural New England in *The Europeans,* urban New York in *Washington Square,* Venice in *The Aspern Papers,* London in *The Princess Casamassima,* and Paris, not only as a word, but as an exhalation in *The Ambassadors.* Raw Americans and initiated Americans moved upon this sufficient stage with all their mortality hanging about them, all the comic or tragic signs of their peculiarity.

Their nationality marks them, and their exemption from the economic struggle marks them. His people are not only American (or English or French or Italian), they are specifically and complexly so. Their special, national types sound variations upon the theme. National attitudes to the freedom allowed the unmarried girl, to marriage, to money, to religion, to various problems of the personal life, all have their say. And for added richness he gave the counterpoint of one viewpoint clashing with another, the American with the English, the English with the French, and so on. He achieved the impression of layer upon layer of opinion, of belief, of creed, held by the nation, by the class within the nation, and by the sentient individual within the class.

Particularly, his series of novels given up entirely to the Eng-

lish scene have about them an effluence of thickness. In these
novels, *The Princess Casamassima, The Spoils of Poynton, The
Tragic Muse, The Awkward Age, What Maisie Knew,* and *The
Sacred Fount,* as he had in the early American novels, James
showed that the national contrasts were not necessary; that all
the agreements and conflicts necessary for his story were wrapped
richly one upon the other in any thick society. Thickness meant
the rapture (for the author) of things one must do and not do and
all the resultant rewards and penalties. It meant live characters,
for it meant characters struggling. Social prescription and the
complement of departure from the rules made up the ground
level of his stories. James gloried in inhibitions and restraints.
For then the spontaneous vitality of his heroes had something
strong, definite, and inimical to push against. In his typical hero
there is a pulse of energy opposed, dammed up, bursting out,
or forcefully pushed down.

In any treatment of the personal life which is also a treatment of the social scene, there would seem to be two poles of interest: first, the manner in which the character represents his
age, his nation, his class; and second, the manner in which the
character is a being, an individual. Yet analysis breaks down in
application to any novel with the breath of life in it. James'
people are alive in all their attributes, whether social or personal, and one cannot tear one symptom from the other without damaging the personality.

The young man from St. Louis in *Watch and Ward* represents
perhaps the East's uneasy idea of the whole, wild, Western
frontier. Yet he is not a type but a particular, insolent, attractive opportunist. Gilbert Osmond, the Italianate American in
The Portrait of a Lady, had come to be a conscious expatriate,
more European than the Europeans, the conventional man par
excellence. Yet one hates a man in Osmond, not a type. One
resents the particular snobbery, not a type of snobbery.

Adam Verver in *The Golden Bowl,* inexpressive and heavy
with the power of great wealth, represents, perhaps, the elemental weight of possessions. Yet he is a man in a predicament, and
one does not pity the type but the man. Isabel Archer, Osmond's
victim, is not only the epitome and symbol of the new American girl, the free, inquiring, flexible, individual woman, she

is Isabel, a particular person, who has a great chance and muffs it. Milly Theale in *The Wings of the Dove* is not only the pitiful type of youth, beauty, energy, and grace who is to die young; she is a particular New York girl who is an orphan, who has red hair, who loves a man who does not love her.

In order to uncover the mechanics of his characters' existence, to find out how they live, what they do with their time, where they go but not what they mean, one could, for the purpose, divorce action from theme and simply exhibit a few of his people in their movements.

In *Roderick Hudson,* for instance, Rowland Mallet has money and likes pictures and statues. In Northampton, Massachusetts, he comes upon an unsuitable law student, Roderick Hudson. Rowland does not work for a living but has a good income by inheritance from a Puritan sea captain of a father. He transplants the young man, who has shown a more than amateur talent for sculpture, to Rome to give him a chance to grow. Without a bad conscience at all, Roderick launches himself and his story upon Rowland's money.

In *The Portrait of a Lady,* Ralph Touchett is a wealthy young man, unfit through illness for either work or play. He has kindness and wit and takes a fancy to his cousin, Isabel Archer, a penniless, independent-minded young woman who has come abroad under his mother's care. In due course, in an extraordinary interview with his dying father, Ralph arranges that his own inheritance be reduced to a pittance and the greater part of it be left to Isabel. Ralph has an impulse to see what she will make of herself, with monetary freedom added to a free disposition. The story is just that—what Isabel does with her money and what the money does with her.

Nick Dormer in *The Tragic Muse* likes to paint pictures, but family pride, inertia, and sex seem certain to make for the conforming life. In the first place his dead father was an important Parliamentary figure of the preceding generation. His mother has the habit of rule and demands that Nick be a dutiful son to a dead father and stand for office. Also, old Mr. Carteret, a friend of the powerful dead father, waves checks, figuratively, in Nick's path. In addition, temptation, in the form of a beautiful, political cousin, Julia Dallow, plagues the susceptible Nick.

Julia, while demanding his conformity, offers as a suitable reward her hand in marriage. The surprising fact that Nick flies in the face of tradition, money, and sex and settles for art makes him an exception and also a modest hero. His course is made possible, the author makes clear, not only by nerve and idealism, but by a small, independent income. His entry into Bohemia and his connection with Miriam Rooth, the actress, grow out of his valuable independence.

Milly Theale in *The Wings of the Dove* has money. Kate Croy has not. They both love young Merton Densher, a moneyless but clever newspaperman. The idea of the story lives in Milly's reactions to her knowledge of her own imminent death. But the movement of the story, from Switzerland, to England, to Italy, and its splendor of setting are due to the fortune over which so much deadly skirmishing takes place.

James' characters have room to commit sins upon a large scale. Roderick's story takes him very quickly out of New England, to Rome, and then to Florence. He ends story and life in Switzerland. He has been, in the meantime, on a liberal tour of studios, cathedrals, and art galleries. Isabel Archer looks about Europe as James had. She sees what she can of Italy as well as England, and her cruel disillusionment takes place in a renovated palace in Rome.

Nick Dormer's troubles come upon him in varying bright scenes: a great industrial and artistic exhibit in Paris, the ordered confusion of a rural election in England, the celebration of electoral victory in Julia's large and beautiful country house. His withdrawal from public splendor into Miriam's world makes him a special case. Milly Theale's life and the certain shortness of it moves in a pathetic pageant across Europe. Her money has pitched her drama into the glare of privilege and extravagance; its stages include London dinner parties, country-house festivities, and, at the end, death in a Venetian palazzo.

The circumstances are made by money and privilege. Yet these are the superficialities of his novels. With money shuffled out of the way as a difficulty, his characters have the time and the energy for every other kind of pitfall, whether moral or aesthetic. On the surface, on the basis of a hardhearted sketch of the life contained in one or another of his novels, it might seem doubtful that

James' stories pulse with the true and undeniable sense of life. One sometimes wonders why. The world he has staked out as his own is only a tiny corner of life. It resolves itself into that atypical bit of society which in the late nineteenth century and early twentieth century, in a period between wars, lived a life of leisure and affluence. It was a traveling, party-giving, distinction-making, art-knowing group, at the furthest remove from the dirt and sweat of the common lot. It was artificial because most educated in manner, a group in which the queerest twists of tradition had hardened into social law. That there is life here is James' great success.

In order to measure the extent of James' world, I have made the previous discussion descriptive rather than critical. I have behaved as if James were literally a reporter of the social scene rather than a storyteller. Now, the viewpoint should shift. He could not, simply through knowledge of his world and the will to report it, make good fiction. Fiction is different in kind from history: "the actual is not the true," as James' friend, Louis Stevenson, said. Without discussing the style or artistic means in general (to be taken up later), one could try to show that he was accurate yet never literal. His private domain was the world of society, but in his pages it was society transformed into a kind of fable, which was potent with life, yet significant in form.

James was a close observer of life. But he was the master of the facts he gathered in. He had a high, free way with them. He thought that the deadly addition of one fact to another in a vast stack led fiction to a dead end. In an article, *The New Novel,* published in 1914, he stated as his opinion that the so-called "slice-of-life" method gave the reader merely "all the entertainment that can come from watching a wayfarer engage with assurance in an alley that we know to have no issue—and from watching for the sake of the face that he may show on reappearing at its mouth." He held with a bold, not a careful, verisimilitude. Selection of the salient detail and omission of every unnecessary or gratuitous item was his method.

For, in the first place, he admitted no detail to the story which did not smell of his idea. He did not necessarily cripple himself by the manner in which he left out. He built by the use of convention. If convention is the means of telling truth by a lie, it is the means by which his art, or any art, preserves and perpetuates such life as the artist knows.

James varied a great deal in practice as to how much of the gross detail of life and living he put into his stories. In the stories written before his trip to Europe in 1869, he was a clever observer of the modest life. Such early tales as *Poor Richard, A Landscape Painter,* and *A Day of Days,* are sound but pallid. The same stricture holds true of the novels *Watch and Ward* and even of the greater *Washington Square.* It is always deceptive to generalize as to periods in an author's work, but it does seem true to say that a difference in tone can be observed in the novels, *Roderick Hudson* and *The American,* written as a direct result of his first full impression of the Old World. They are full of a new confidence and a new youthfulness and yet are perhaps too little connected with the facts of life.

During the middle period of his writing, the time of the novel of revolution, *The Princess Casamassima,* the novel of reform, *The Bostonians,* and the novel of the theater, *The Tragic Muse,* he seemed to be making more of a conscious effort to be broad, to be more inclusive of the knobby facts of existence. Yet growing in him even in that period was the desire to convert, to represent by analogy, which tendency had its culmination in the last great novels, *The Wings of the Dove, The Ambassadors,* and *The Golden Bowl.* While these last novels are less broad and less realistic in the straightforward manner of *The Princess* and *The Bostonians,* they succeed in conveying a sense of life by a difficult and mature fusion of the romance of the early novels with the sense of the depths of human nature broached in the middle group. He gained power toward the end simply by his increasing use of convention.

The most extreme case of the suppression of fact as flat-footed fact is in *The Sacred Fount,* a novel of the year 1901, just precedent to the group by which he is best known. While it is a smaller thing than the later novels, it shows well the difference between the literal reporting of the social scene and the artist's making over that scene into something rich and strange.

The scene of *The Sacred Fount* is an English week end at a country house. The characters are a handful of guests. What previous lives his guests have led, who their host is, where they will go and what they will do after their week-end holiday is over, what are their sources of income, what is their religion, their politics, their preferences in art or amusement: all these are questions he leaves rigidly alone. The pairs of guests, strolling within the house or outside under the trees of Newmarch, meeting, retreating, losing and overtaking one another, exchanging partners in ballet style, have, despite their remoteness from common life, a frightening aliveness. The novel is a gruesome fairy tale about the kind of rapacious vitality which two members of the party possess.

These two are what they are, youthful and brilliant, at the direct, moral expense of another soul, one of a husband, one of a mistress. They virtually siphon off their partners' lifeblood and in consequence lead freer and fuller lives. As the fortunate one increases in life, the generous partner decreases, one from youth into old age, the other from brilliant charm into feeble disconnectedness. It is a parable of the use people make of each other, and it intrudes its ugly miracle into a worldly scene without injuring the generally witty and satirical tone. The story succeeds without the props by which stories usually live. It shows the means by which several characteristic literary devices of the author could make over raw material into fiction.

This short novel is a mixture of realism and poetry. Yet all inappropriate relations are conventionalized out of existence. A handful of characters simply spend the week end at a large country place and make out each other's secrets.

Omission is the first device: the ruthless suppression of irrelevant fact, a means of dramatic compression sufficiently indicated. The second convention is related to the first, the sense of all that is understood among the characters as to life and living. Their conversation does not explain their background, but it does indicate attitudes from which the reader might infer the total, complicated fabric of late nineteenth and early twentieth century life. These people carry round them the aura of empire, class, and privilege. Their slightest witticism reveals the whole of their world. The third convention is that of the observer through whose mind the entire story filters. What he does not see, the reader does not see; what he does see, the reader sees. He is outside the main action, yet near enough to be scorched. James risks a danger in this story in the circumstance that his narrator quails so under the weight of his discoveries that he begins to doubt his own sanity. But it is not through this convention of the point of view that the author almost topples his story.

Another device, used here to excess, endangers the unity of the impression. The device is that of the kind of dialogue employed. For conversation, in James, is a device. It is of an unequaled boldness and complexity. It is more intense, more vital, not less so, than it is possible to be in a careful imitation of real talk. It serves to illuminate character and to push and drive action when used successfully. Yet in the last one hundred pages of *The Sacred Fount* it becomes an excess. The book is that much longer for the sake of a brilliant, tortuous, midnight talk between the narrator and one of his observed ones. The flaw in this case is that the action has been settled already to the satisfaction of the reader, and that this conversation in no wise changes the outcome.

The particular failure only proves the case. James understood his task, which was not just the job of observing and reporting life, but a different kind of work, the magician's job of transforming life. The work completed is then, somehow, truer, but also a new world, one of its own kind. Its connections with the real world are all disguised and subterranean. Truth flows from life to art through hidden channels but suffers a change upon the way. Experience becomes not less true but more true, crystal clear, fixed, definite, and permanent. The work of Henry James in all his stories was to fulfill this peculiar law of fiction.

PART *Three*

Theme: The Collision
of the Individual and Society

IF JAMES' FIELD IS THE GREAT WORLD, HIS "WORLD" SHINES with a light that it has nowhere else. For in the minds of his heroes and heroines the "world" has meanings and excitements that the ordinary member of society knows not at all. There follow three samples of the characteristic excitement which society provides for the Jamesian hero.

Roderick Hudson attends a studio party in Rome and marks an epoch in his life. A few months before he had been a discontented law student in the desert waste of New England; now he is the favorite young man of the arts in Rome. He has completed a statue and knows the work to be good. He believes in himself and trembles at the knowledge of sure fame, of sure glory. No matter that there are grumblings upon the outskirts and complaints made of a too easy success. Roderick has the foolhardiness of his youth. He drinks too much, talks too much, and proclaims himself irresistibly. At this pitch of exaltation the joy-intoxicated young man perches for a moment.

That is one social occasion in a James novel. The reader smiles at the naïve young man but smiles with him and is caught up with him into tremulous enthusiasm.

Another social occasion, notable for its enlargement within the mind of the hero, is Hyacinth's visit to the Princess' country house in the climactic center of *The Princess Casamassima.* To anyone of her world, to anyone but Hyacinth himself, the incident in itself would be as prosaic, as usual, and as limited in

49

meaning as Christina's desires. To him, the occasion is painful with ecstasy.

He vibrates with circle upon circle of ideas shaken free within him by his own imaginative recognitions. He has escaped at last out of the black London streets. He has forgotten, for the moment, revolution. He has entered into that great world to which he is a pledged enemy. Every stifled nerve of his body responds to it with gratitude. Starved for luxury, he finds that he has a faculty for enjoying it. He responds to its various forms with mental rather than physical abandonment.

At Medley, the house, the garden, and its mistress speak to him of beauty for which he has had a lifelong nostalgia. Yet Hyacinth merely walks in the garden, drives in the country, explores the old house, and feasts in solitude upon its books and prints, caressing them with hand and eye. He seems to please Christina, but he does not try to understand her. He knows that the house is rented, that his being there is a whim, that Christina, perhaps, is playing with him, and that he, himself, is ridiculous in his enchantment. But his imagination responds to his surroundings in a sense of coming home, of being enfranchised of the world. He has added the love of life to the hatred of it and made his mind the scene of irreconcilable conflicts.

In the author's greatest story, Milly Theale's, in *The Wings of the Dove,* there is, near the beginning, a pivotal chapter whose subject is the description of a London dinner party. What follows is more than a satire of manners, for the heroine is an intruder. Milly sees beneath the conventional items of behavior at Mrs. Lowder's party into a dizzying significance. In the midst of the passing of dishes, in the seconds between snatches of gossip with her right-hand neighbor, she was a prevision of her fate. She hesitates for a second between flight and involvement, for involvement in this set promises crosscurrents of the rich and the deep, of the sinister and the divided among these people who reach out to her to take her in, for her charm and for her money. At a common, heavy-mannered dinner, Milly has all at once come upon what strikes her as life at its thickest and most suggestive to her uninitiated, wayward individuality. The sinister is as yet a faint taste, while the general mixture served up to her is pleasant in its exhilaration. The limping name of social success could be applied to what she saw that she was to achieve here. But its meaning was to be coextensive with the reach of her imagination.

The flat social occasion is not what it seems. In the mind of a Roderick, a Hyacinth, or a Milly, each one of whom sees the social world from the outside, as a stranger might, the worldly occasion is a provocation. It provokes a special quality of imagination which takes nothing as given, which tests each experience upon the individual truth, for which each experience is unique.

The very act of comprehension, of imaginative penetration in marking relationships, in noting contradictions, in seizing upon occult meanings causes a dangerous exhilaration of the mind. The daring ego, testing nothing except upon its own ringing truth, makes the natural mistake of identifying as part of itself that great world spread before it. In this mood each enlargement of the personal life seems to flow outward from the self. The world in the beauty of its form and arrangement seems to shape itself to please.

In each case, Roderick's, Hyacinth's, or Milly's, there is a momentary illusion of power. The splendor of insight has persuaded the will that it, too, holds the scene in bondage. It follows that the opposite movement, that of contraction into the knowledge of things as they are, convinces the hero of the fact of the separateness of the world from himself. Its persons and its objects are distinct realities, not playthings of his fancy and his will. The two movements, the bellows movement of expansion into a sense of glory and contraction into a sense of reality, make the two hinges of the action. The climax is that moment of the extreme reach of the hero's proud assumption, the assumption which, at that instant, is pierced by reality.

The quality of mind which permits the hero to be so open to the assault of the world, to be so exposed, is the quality that saves him. In the end it floats him through disillusionment and past it to a clear seeing of the whole.

Roderick is brought low to see his fatuousness in a failure of hand and nerve. His nose is rubbed in his obtuseness, and so, without issue, he walks off his cliff in Switzerland. Yet he does it so handsomely, so gracfully, so romantically (with the unashamed romance of James' early novels), that for the spectator, his wronged friend, his deserted fiancée, and the aggravated reader, he carries his career to an end with no loss of the essential Hudson flourish.

Hyacinth, too, is persuaded by life of the impossible nature of his trouble. He loses everything, both the right to destroy and the right to enjoy life. Roughly, without any of Hudson's swagger, he died a suicide. Even at the end, something of what Hyacinth saw and felt and succeeded in being in his great city stays and will not scatter. What he carried about in his mind seems more substantial than all the rest.

Milly, too, loses in every particular. Her world contracts to a short, sharp wait for the grave, and it contracts into the ugly truth of knowing herself deceived by friend and lover. She has gone up and she has come down. Yet for her deceivers, Milly, even dead, means a power and a beauty which transcends her history. It leaves the victory tasteless: "We shall never be again as we were!" they repeat face to face.

The worldly occasion opens out as idea to the James hero or heroine and takes on a meaning out of all proportion to the actual event. This could not happen to the person made by that society. His protagonist must be, in essence, an outsider, one able to seize upon the shape of the world and see it whole, play with it as a symbol even while embroiling himself in it. The nature of the principal character in the novels is that of a conscious, exploring imagination, with the social and human phenomena of the "world" as the field of exploration. An initiate would not serve, since he, the man or woman, tailored by his world, was born and reared to take that world on trust. James must have the best of both worlds, the splendid forms of the old, and the unpredictable energy of the new. Society as an objective reality and, in juxtaposition, the making, shaping individual will: these are the explosive elements of his mixture.

The nature of the hero affects the total meaning of the author's work. For James sees life and reports it in terms of the intrusion of the strange element, the individual, into the world. The world is in some way made different, and, of course, comically, tragically, the nature of the person too is affected. In order to see this tug of war for what it is, one should try to understand what kind of a person James' hero is.

The author's antithesis to his renowned complexity is his courageous use of the simple. He is not afraid of emphasis: by its use he anchors and makes fast a multiplicity of development. Striking story idea and exceptional hero rivet the mind upon the fundamentals while leaving the writer free to make of them what he will. About James' gift for narrative it is enough at present to say that the germ idea of each novel is of such a seizable nature as to command the reader's attention throughout its development. As to his principal characters, he prefers the superlative to the average.

James created a gallery of exceptional men and women. Among the creatures of his imagination he proposed the following: the most gifted American artist (Roderick Hudson), the true type of the American (Christopher Newman), the most beautiful woman (Christina Light), the type of revolutionary leader (Paul Muniment), the greatest actress (Miriam Rooth), the richest girl (Milly Theale), and others of the same reverberating importance. He asserts the eminence of these persons and carries off their grandness with the interested assent of the reader.

Great talent marks Roderick and Miriam; beauty, Christina; and money, Milly Theale and Maggie Verver. They live in the eye of the world. Yet even his heroes and heroines who have no such distinguishing mark set upon them have, each one, had an experience which makes them striking and exceptional in their own eyes.

Christopher Newman has turned his back upon business. He judges himself to be in a queer kind of crisis when he sets out for Europe. All the events of his story take place in the light of one decisive, remarkable act.

Isabel Archer is taken up by the Touchetts, and, as a consequence, her life becomes a sequence of interesting choices. Isabel in Florence is not the Isabel her aunt had discovered in the empty family house in Albany.

Hyacinth Robinson meets his Princess. Nothing can ever be quite ordinary again. Verena Tarrant moves into Olive Chancellor's house on Beacon Street. Every happening which follows upon this action has a kind of theatrical glare. Even the most private adventures, Maisie's trip to Boulogne with Lord Claude,

Fleda Vetch's stay at Poynton, Nanda's brief "time," as she calls it, in society; Lambert Strether's grateful absorption of Europe in the Paris of Marie de Vionnet—all these personal excitements have the mark of the unique, if not for the world, at least for the persons to whom they occur. Each one of these individuals is lifted out of his ordinary existence. Each one is presented with a horizon opened out, widened, lifted in an unprecedented way. The personal life has become rich, strange, and difficult.

Whether the adventure takes place on a public stage or a private one, the person who is the central character is equipped by his creator with the temperament for the adventure. James is in one sense writing about convention, but all his heroes and heroines are unconventional.

The initiation of the drama is the attempt by the individual to be someone or other than the person his particular society desires him to be:

a) Roderick Hudson takes it upon himself to be an artist, and not just a New England lawyer and simple support for his mother.

b) Isabel Archer decides to exercise her intelligence in a free choice of her future rather than accept the first presented suitor.

c) Hyacinth Robinson chooses to be a revolutionist, and then, in flat contradiction, a connoisseur of the high life, of art, and of love, rather than a good, industrious bookbinder.

d) Nick Dormer resigns his seat in Parliament and breaks with his ambitious fiancée simply to paint portraits.

e) Milly Theale defies her worst enemy, death, and resolves to live out her life at the pitch she chooses rather than die as a tame victim.

f) Lambert Strether, coming to Europe to admonish, stays to appreciate. He quits his old precautionary self to find enlargement and beauty in what he has called sin.

g) Ralph Pendrel declines to live in this world. He steps entirely out of it and into one of his own creating.

Not only the striking circumstance but the striking personality clears away the debris of common life. These people live in an air of exceptional choices. Their crises are large ones, and the pressures ranged against them arouse greatness of emotion in response.

James is marked by this very difference between himself and his contemporaries. In his novels the principal character is a true hero. It is not too farfetched to place James' stories in relation to the stories in the English Renaissance drama. He is the only modern novelist who bears even a wry modern reference to that attitude and that manner. Although the lives of his principals are grounded in the actualities of the 1870's the 1880's, the 1890's, and the early 1900's, their stories are, in structure and in effect, large and bold, exceptional stories of exceptional people.

The hero or heroine, to whom that name can be rightly applied, lives in special isolation from the common lot, just as the kings of Shakespeare lived. The advantage of the overweighted, top-heavy social structure (the advantage for the writer) is then evident. It gave James a large social stage and it gave him heroes and villains to move upon it. They are marked by leisure and money rather than by privilege and power, but these attributes brand them effectively.

Yet one should note that James' understanding of the tragic idea is not altogether the classic understanding. His hero is a tragic hero in the sense that his story has a large, uncluttered stage and that he himself is of decisive proportions as an individual. But the manner of his downfall is curious and modern and in part a divergence from the traditional idea of tragedy.

The author gains strength and dignity through his kinship to the Elizabethans by placing evil as a positive, breathing presence in the center of his situation. But he is curious and modern in that he creates a division between the hero as good and another character or group of characters as evil. His hero is a person in whom virtue is a positive, imaginative force to whom evil things are done. He shows the real and effective difference between positive good and positive bad, but he apportions these qualities between person and person. He fails to show the tragic flaw, as the Greek drama had and Shakespeare had, as a rift splitting open one human being. This is perhaps James' greatest weakness. Yet he almost overcomes the effect that this lack might have in his work by the great plausibility of his characters, both the "good" and the "bad." Also, James discovers under one's eyes how goodness is a temptation, and sometimes a willful provocation, to evil. This aspect of truth seems so just and striking in him that its trueness in part blots out the effect of his really central weakness.

For the purpose of the immediate discussion, it is enough to point out the heroic scale of his presentation and the fact that it gives an enduring interest to his work, denied to many of his earnest contemporaries who worked altogether in the naturalist vein.

To succeed, James' heroic scale of living and feeling had to build upon a foundation of solid reality. There had to be, and James successfully placed there, a recognizable sill of things as they are. It is his great strength that the reality keeps pace with the grandness. The heroes of the last novels, the Strethers, the Millys, and the Maggies, are motivated more specifically and exactly than the heroes of the earlier, simpler novels. But throughout his career James consistently granted his protagonists largeness of conception, boldness of action, and freedom of gesture.

If the hero of the novels initiates his drama by performing an act in defiance of convention or by being in a state of mind which cuts across the grain of the social pattern, he keeps it going by continuing to be the unpredictable person in the predictable society. James must be understood in this sense despite the fact that his Isabels and Millys are not obvious rebels but think themselves joyous participants. It is only when Isabel or Milly thinks for a moment that she has won a personal conquest over her world that the monster shows itself. She realizes then that society has a law of its own which is not necessarily her law.

In this drama of the ego, this bellows movement of expansion and contraction, the individual who is the center of the movement stands exposed. For one reason or another, which James is careful to relate to the actual, real conditions of living, the hero is, and must be, for the drama, uninitiated. The opposing characters have an advantage over the hero of knowledge of the world and the habit of adept practice in its games. For the author's cruel purposes, the hero must not know his way, must always feel for it and find it for himself. He must be seen by the reader, for the pity and terror of it, to be stepping unknowing onto dangerous ground, always threatened and never safe.

The "world," on the other hand, in the eyes of the newcomer, must, again for the drama, be a positive and beautiful temptation, an invitation to his inmost being to grow and flower. In attaching the attention and sympathy of the reader to his hero, James has had to objectify and make real the aspects of the world which so attract that person. In part the reader is led to see through the eyes of the uninitiated. He feels the compulsion of the world as the hero does. Yet he has the double vision, and in terror sees the pitfalls dug for the unwary. Thus, the author-god of this drama sets up a vibration inside the spectator which operates with increasing force as the consciousness of the Hyacinth or the Maggie of the situation explores and expands, and at last explosively sees. The reader awaits with painful tension the growth of that consciousness until it skyrockets into coincidence with his own.

James' entire work forms an ascending scale of complication in his illustration of his theme, the collision of the individual and organized society. He begins with simple, outward differences and goes into greater and greater involvement of the imagination and judgment (which are one in him). At the end he turns upon himself and achieves massive simplicity in the midst of complexity.

The spiral of significance begins with the national divergence of the American and the European, develops into the more essential contrast of innocence and experience, grows into the mature idea of the complementary nature of character and culture, and finally, the halving of the world into energy and form. But it is a sort of violence to extract idea from story. The idea lives in the story, in its action and passion. But in every situation which he treats, one can discern that James has said another word upon the problem of the individual and his existence in a difficult world. Five aspects of the perennial idea can be detached and examined: (*a*) the American in Europe; (*b*) innocence and experience; (*c*) the underprivileged in society; (*d*) the artist in society; (*e*) the estrangement from society.

The American is a walking metaphor of the writer's basic obsession. He is a foreigner, a new man in an old world, one against many, a classless person in a class society, the individual entangled in a tradition. A single figure torn out of a background (America) which had offered him no support, he has come abroad to the new field of endeavor (Europe), a rich complex of good and evil. Here, as an exile, he wanders in a garden of marvelous adventure.

Before commenting on James' development of his theme in these American-in-Europe stories, one should interject here something of his subjective problem, his backhanded regard for his own kind.

On his decisive trip to Europe in 1869 and 1870, James awoke not only to Europe, but to America. It was as if Europe made him see the essential quality of his own country. Whenever he made a European observation, he referred it to an American one. His mind from that date oscillated between two poles. A part of his amusement in writing was to bring the two vibrating opposites together in one picture. As he matured, the national characteristics merged into and came to stand for human ones. Yet he used the obvious, national contrasts again and again, even when he saw them as metaphors. To the end of his career he drew vivacity and vitality out of the shock and clash of national temperament.

The twenty-seven-year-old Henry James was aggravated as well as delighted with the strength of his impressions. He wrote sharp notes home to relatives and friends who were living and working in Ulysses S. Grant's America. That year the sight of his countrymen abroad provoked the following:

A set of people less framed to provoke national self-complacency than the latter it would be hard to imagine. There is but one word to use in regard to them—vulgar, vulgar, vulgar. Their ignorance— their stingy, defiant, grudging attitude towards everything European —their perpetual reference of all things to some American standard or precedent which exists only in their own unscrupulous wind-bags —and then our unhappy poverty of voice, of speech and of physiognomy—these things glare at you hideously. On the other hand, we seem a people of *character,* we seem to have energy, capacity and intellectual stuff in ample measure. What I have pointed at as our vices are the elements of the modern man with *culture* quite left out. It's the absolute and incredible lack of *culture* that strikes you in common travelling Americans.

In 1874, he wrote from Florence:

But pity our poor bare country and don't revile. England and Italy, with their countless helps to life and pleasure, are the lands for happiness and self-oblivion. It would seem that in our great unendowed, unfurnished, unentertained and unentertaining continent, where we all sit sniffing, as it were, the very earth of our foundations, we ought to have leisure to turn out something handsome from the heart of simple human nature.

One should add to these quotations the humorous discourse by a character in *The Point of View* on the serious need in America of a little honest coarseness, which the country lacked, in place of the overnice vulgarity which it had in abundance.

James held his countrymen in a loving disrespect, yet he chose his heroes and heroines from among them. He had a theory that if an American was anyone at all, he was more of a person altogether than the corresponding European. Starting from a lower level, making himself a person in the face of various odds, he had to have flexibility, "moral spontaneity," "intellectual grace."

The peculiar inner development is put to extreme tests. As Americans in Europe, these accomplished individuals are intruders, even while desiring to be participants. America had seemed to them barren of social development, so coming abroad meant for them the importance of a migration from a thin to a thick culture. At home their energy had spilled and wasted. All the pressure had been their own, pushing out and failing to find worthy resistance. Now, in Europe, the pressure had turned upon them. History, ancient and contemporary, traditions, customs, objects, peoples, all crowd them. The result of the pressure, says the author by implication, is the more perfect, painful shaping of the individual.

The series of stories of Americans in Europe has been understood in an inadequate fashion as a picture of the victimization of the simple individual by the corrupt society. It is true that certain of his characters have the appearance of sacrificial lambs, Daisy Miller and Francie Dosson, for instance. Each one, in the perfection of innocence, falls into the obvious traps of a jaded society: Daisy by her unchaperoned picnic on a Swiss lake, and Francie, who is the heroine of *The Reverberator*, by meeting in a Paris park a gentleman other than her fiancé. Daisy's and

Francie's valiant honesty does not save them, only hurts them. The spirit with which they defy the enemy to think the worst only sinks them deeper in the eyes of those onlookers who have been delicately schooled in depravity. James makes this moral obtuseness appear as something horrible as well as comic. The equipment to weigh and judge, which European centuries had molded into a fine instrument, is set vibrating and pointing to wrong conclusions by one pretty, pathetic young girl. One should note the fact that in each case the agent of condemnation is a fellow American of Daisy's and Francie's. Even in these light stories, James' judgment cuts both ways.

One should remember, too, that victimization works both ways. The most triumphant turnabout of this theme is the story of Chad Newsome and Marie de Vionnet in *The Ambassadors*. In this novel the young American is the cruel exploiter, and the older, experienced European woman is the gentle victim.

Other American exploiters are the vital barbarian, Mrs. Headway, in *The Siege of London,* and the flexible rascal, Scott Homer, in *Mrs. Medwin.* These are two Americans who come out well at the top of the European social heap. And in *Lady Barberina* the English heroine is as pitiful a sufferer in America as Daisy and Francie had been in Europe. Her hard confident American husband as thoroughly misunderstands her as the Europeans had misunderstood the American girls.

Victimization is only the obvious face of the story. Other, more knowing Americans go abroad with brave intentions. Europe, as the complex of thickness representing "life" for James, proves too much for the talented, the intelligent, and the good. The artist Roderick Hudson chokes on the quantity of inspiration available in Rome; Isabel chooses the wrong husband out of a superfluity of applicants who offer themselves to her in England and in Italy; and Maggie finds the worst fortune enshrined in what had seemed unbeatable felicity.

Below the tragicomedy of misunderstanding and misjudgment in these national contrasts and clashes is a profound theme. James' American in Europe is attempting to complete himself, to find a fit extension of the self in the outer world. He is a person searching for a habitation. Yet his native freedom makes him one who breaks the mold to which he is trying to adapt himself.

He finds out its cracks and flaws as easily as Maggie finds the fault in the golden bowl.

The movement from America to Europe has different names for each individual: for Newman it signifies the exchange of barrenness for profusion; for Isabel, the exchange of ignorance for knowledge; for Lambert Strether, the exchange of Puritanism for a sense of joy.

He, the middle-aged hero of *The Ambassadors*, is almost the best, as he is almost the last, of James' American heroes. He has the damning gift of a moral sense that is identical with his imagination. Europe turns his imagination on as it had never been turned on before in all his fifty-odd years of doing as others had desired in his native, "good," and all too restrictive Boston.

Paris makes all the difference for Strether. He who had crossed the ocean as an ambassador to reprimand and order home an erring son stays on to savor that boy's Paris. He accomplishes an enlargement of sympathy and a sharpening of judgment in the air of the wonderful city. He has a late-blooming youth in an expansion into new modes of living.

Then, when he perceives the justice of the situation, that Chad Newsome, the young man he has been sent out to rescue, is perfectly self-sufficient, and that the woman in the situation, Marie de Vionnet, is the afflicted and suffering victim, Strether's education is complete. He turns on Chad and gives him a solemn and damning curse for any present or future movement of desertion. The circle is finished. Strether has seen what enjoyment could be and what damnation could be. He has thrown his fervor into the scale for a particular outcome. Yet he is down, not up, as a result of his enlightenment. He is the chief victim of the story by becoming its chief actor.

In so far as the American has been deprived, he is dramatic in his accessions of insight and power. He was almost the only man of James' time who could be shown as mature and thoughtful and yet shown taking the whole composite of culture and society to himself in one gesture of acceptance. The enlightenment which comes, as it must to any completed individual, is a double-edged weapon. He suffers from it to the extent that he gains.

The characteristic movement of the American is from west to east, but in the unfinished novel *The Ivory Tower* James broke new ground. Here the excitement is that of a return after a withdrawal. Graham Fielder brings back culture to the money society. By the magnanimous whim of his millionaire uncle, the young man is to inherit a fortune. The unfinished novel was to exhibit him as the man of culture, retaking his rightful, prominent place in the powerful American society which had grown and developed in his absence. This is the other side of the medal. James himself, in his own person, in 1905, had made the return, but death prevented him from giving this counter-movement complete expression in a novel.

Just as James was capable of seeing all of life condensed into the adventures of an American in Europe, he could see it through another of his novelist's windows as the experience of a child, or a young girl, first entering into the activity of organized society.

Youth is one of James' touchstones for the world. It weighs society and finds it lacking and is put in the balance, a sacrifice that adds somehow to the total. Inexperience is a kind of foreignness. This theme overlaps with the one just treated, that of the American in Europe, for many of these Americans are young and add the hazard of youth to that of strangeness. One thinks of Daisy Miller, of arrogant Roderick, and of Isabel, Milly, and Maggie. Yet the special Jamesian necessity for looking at life through fiction as the picture of youth growing into experience, of pliability becoming independence dates from his earliest novel, *Watch and Ward,* which is an entirely American story. And as good examples of the idea can be drawn from altogether European stories which are exempt from the distraction of national distinctions. The three examples to follow are all of the other side of the Atlantic: Morgan Moreen in *The Pupil,* Maisie Farrange in *What Maisie Knew,* and Nanda Brookenham in *The Awkward Age.* The characters in *The Pupil* are American but all sunk so deep in Europe that America is hardly even a memory.

To meet James' purposes, each of the three, Morgan, Maisie, and Nanda, must be comparatively helpless. They are all young, Morgan, an adolescent boy with a weak heart; Maisie, a little girl; and Nanda, a very young and inexperienced woman. Morgan's shame comes to him through his family. He discovers that his people, mother, father, brother, and sisters, are dishonest as well as shabby. Maisie's difficulty is in discovering who constitutes her family. Although a divorce court had awarded her to Papa and Mama alternately for each six months of the year, she finds each time a Papa and a Mama less and less willing to receive her. Nanda, kept out of sight as long as possible by a young mother, has the misfortune to love the same man as the competent mother. Thus, each one of these has before him or her a moral stumbling block of giant size.

The world takes nimble advantage of Morgan, Maisie, and Nanda. The world, as Morgan's family, while taking a queer sort of pride in him and his cleverness—he is their little freak —unloads all responsibility for the boy upon a penniless tutor. Maisie's parents successively kiss her and wash their hands of her. Nanda's mother blackens her daughter's name by instancing her own badness as a ruinous influence upon a young, impressionable girl, until Nanda says of herself: "I shall be one of those people who don't . . . I shall be . . . one of those who haven't."

The worst has been done to them. Wise parents, friends, lovers, holding every easy advantage of age, experience, practice, have had their way. Yet the result is not clear as a victory for them. The part taken by Morgan, Maisie, and Nanda has made a difference in the proportions of the whole. By placing the disturbing innocence of a child or a young person in the center of a corrupt group and letting us watch the result, James demonstrates several truths about the individual and society.

The child, shown as the most helpless member of the group, deceived, used, discarded, yet somehow acts to scatter the other members out of their accustomed orbits. Each one of the three is the essential Jamesian individual, an expanding, growing, fervent ego, reaching out to life and the display of life offered. The older members of the group are gathered round watching this groping movement of the weakest member. When the expansive, delicate growth threatens at any point some possession or some pretension of theirs, they then adopt subtle means to stop that movement. In the effort they wound not only the child, but each other and themselves.

Yet James does justice to the beautiful world. He shows that it is good for many things but not for everything. The basic grimness shows its face only occasionally behind the chinks in the bright surface. The texture and tone have the wit and the lightness of the best days and best moments of the most perfect citizens of the world. *The Pupil* moves for the most part in the atmosphere of satire and "fun"—Morgan agrees that his parents are amusing—and only drops at unexpected moments into the ugly. Maisie's one devotion, for her amoral stepfather, Lord Claude, has a persuasive tenderness about it that makes black her final good-by to him. Nanda's story, which is a pathetic one, is told in a manner stiff with the expensive, free humor of her mother's circle, whose wildness and abandoned intellectual freedom are given full flavor.

Embedded in these stories of children is a whole philosophy of education. James shows the dangers spread to catch the innocent, and yet he fails to advocate the protection of youth by artificial barriers to knowledge and experience. James is quite Miltonian in his belief that virtue is not virtue which has not been tested, that negative goodness is a poor thing. The moral dusk which surrounds Maisie or Morgan causes their perceptions to "stick fiery off" and their trueness to shine brighter. Nanda, thrown early into the social arena, is contrasted favorably with little Aggie, her friend, who had been educated upon the Italian conventual principal of perfect ignorance held right for young ladies. Once out, into society, little Aggie goes far indeed.

Mr. Longdon, the gentle, rusticated old man who had watched the two girls, as from the sidelines, saw them as "lambs with the great shambles of life in their future; but while one, with its neck in a pink ribbon, and no consciousness but that of being fed from the hand with the small sweet biscuit of unobjectionable knowledge, the other struggled with instincts and forebodings, with the suspicion of its doom and the farborne scent, in the flowery fields, of blood."

It is the strength of the James paradox that so aristocratic a writer, fastidious of every form in life and in art, appreciative of the shaping, refining nature of society should make again and again so basic a democratic contention as the necessity of the freedom of the individual to ruin himself.

Poverty can be as effective an agent for making one a stranger to the social order as foreignness or youthful ingenuousness. James was less acquainted with the distinction of poverty than with the other characteristics named, yet his earliest impressions of London furnished him one classic example of a slums hero. He says in the preface to the 1908 edition of *The Princess Casamassima* that his germ idea for the novel "proceeded quite directly, during the first year of a long residence in London, from the habit and the interest of walking the streets." He had seen the city as an outsider and discovered how wonderful and how awful it was. From thinking how fortunate it was to have doors opened to him, he came to think what it would be to walk those streets and have those doors closed to him. The conception of "some individual sensitive nature or fine mind, some small obscure intelligent creature" was to become Hyacinth Robinson.

Hyacinth had the proper motive for hating the world and the kind of imagination which falls in love with it. At sixteen he had sat down in a library to read straight through the whole file of newspapers telling the lurid story of his father's death at the hands of his mother. He had known for years that the dying Frenchwoman he had been taken to see at Milbank Prison when he was ten, who had so clung to him and frightened him, had been that mother. Now, at sixteen, he had the story whole. The bitterness of his history drove him and his ardent spirit into revolutionary activities. He was fortunate, or unfortunate enough, to be seized upon by one of the real workers of violence as contrasted to the genial dilettantes of discontent. Paul Muniment became the keeper of his conscience and a kind of spiritual director. It was inevitable that with his cachet as a victim of society ("a prostitute's bastard") that he should be given some distinguished and desperate job to perform.

At this point James has pushed his hero as far as desperation will go. There is a limit placed on his existence: it will last only until the order comes to perform an act which he has sworn to do when called upon. Then the author calls in an opposite power to attract in the person of his Princess.

Through her, Hyacinth learns what there is in him which responds to and loves beauty and luxury and freedom. Through her, he enters into the enjoyment of endless refinements of pleasure. (His pleasures are mental and emotional and aesthetic, for he discovers with youthful delight that he is an artist.) James has then his two forces pulling and straining for the true, the veritable Hyacinth. The individual desires to be himself, to be what he is by nature, and to complete that nature by experience. Yet the individual has been claimed.

Since he has been ticketed with such finality, Hyacinth is able to push aside conscientiousness. Tired of living at a pitch of hate, he says: "Isn't it enough now to give my life to the beastly cause . . . without giving my sympathy."

Even before Hyacinth took his fatal oath or met his fatal Princess, he had known that he was in some way different, not only from Pinnie, who had cared for him, and Mr. Vetch, who had first told him that he had a grievance against society, but also different from the revolutionaries Poupin, Schinkel, and even Paul Muniment. Privately, the young man felt a justifiable superiority not only to Pinnie and Mr. Vetch for their weak acquiescence, but to Paul for his stolidity of mind.

What he did not know at first was that he suffered from a difference of imaginative equipment. He had clung to such factitious grounds of superiority as he could. While ashamed of Pinnie's mysterious and sentimental references to the nobility of his father, the idea was a secret prop to his sense of importance. He had known he had a good mind, better than the minds of the deserving people he had sworn to avenge, for

he thought the people in his own class generally very stupid—distinctly what he should call third-rate minds. He wished it hadn't been so, for heaven knew he felt kindly to them and only asked to cast his lot with theirs; but he was obliged to confess that centuries of poverty, of ill-paid toil, of bad insufficient food and wretched housing hadn't a favorable effect on the higher faculties.

But he had added: "Ah when you get to the lowest depths of poverty they may become rich and rare again."

The real ground of his difference became clear to him only after he had stepped for a few days out of the deadly earnestness of Paul's circle. They all suffered from literal-mindedness. It was to the freedom and the figurativeness of the imagination that Hyacinth's Princess appealed. The expansion of the young man's moral and aesthetic powers after his acquaintance with Christina is a spectacle which James had the ability to make intensely and characteristically dramatic. He causes the reader to hang breathless upon each step of Hyacinth's way. This novel is a prime example of James' ability to extract the last bit of excitement from a sudden, explosive opening out of imaginative comprehension.

Hyacinth had discovered himself:

Everything which in a great city could touch the sentient faculty of a youth on whom nothing was lost ministered to his conviction that there was no possible good fortune in life of too "quiet" an order for him to appreciate—no privilege, no opportunity, no luxury to which he mightn't do full justice. It was not so much that he wanted to enjoy as that he wanted to know; his desire wasn't to be pampered but to be initiated.

So he is duly initiated. But what is given to him with one hand is taken away with the other. His friend Paul is no friend, his Princess is false.

The ugly old companion of the Princess, Madame Grandoni, had warned Hyacinth from the first, "Don't give *yourself*. . . ." This is exactly what he had done, not once but twice. First, he had given himself to Paul Muniment, for friendship and for glory. Second, he had given himself to the Princess, for love and for beauty. Both betrayed him, and in the end they betrayed him together. Hyacinth is left a beggar child, with his nose pressed upon the glass of a candy shop.

At this point he is called upon for the fulfillment of his vow. Hyacinth finds that not only have the others betrayed him, he has betrayed himself. His sympathies and beliefs are not his to give. He almost necessarily kills himself. And Mr. Schinkel, a friend, finding him dead, reports the fact quietly to his landlady: "Mr. Robinson has shot himself through the heart. He must have done it while you were fetching the milk."

James was forty-four when he wrote this novel. He had reached full maturity. With good things behind him, he gave himself in this book an even freer range. The social contrasts are broader and the whole field of observation more comprehensive than anything previously attempted. In its social implications James posed a question which he did not answer. He set up both sides with great justice and let them fight for a superior place in the mind of the reader. It would not have bothered him to think that he might have good readers on both sides of the question. He would exact, however, that the good reader should enter imaginatively into his hero's situation and see it as it absolutely is in the novel. There are two insoluble points here, the wrongs of the poor and the rights of a high civilization.

Hyacinth's whole career is a problem of the attempt to find an equilibrium between the claims of life and the claims of art. And he is a representative example of James' obsession with the problem of the opposition of the rights of the individual and the rights of society.

Hyacinth's case as an artist is barely suggested, but many other stories specify the artist's case as that of an almost unassimilable individual in society. The artist must by his very nature be a special problem, both to himself and to the social order. Any adjustment he makes between living and working must be a personal solution. He is therefore a qualified hero for James. As an observer or imitator of life, he is outside it, yet must somehow scrape up a connection with it. And while never of it, he must be so entirely in it as to feel upon his nerves more direct assaults by the world than the ordinary, well rehearsed member.

James is interested in the connections and in the conflicts which arise between art and life at the point of intersection, when the absolute demands of art are at cross-purposes with the absolute demands of society: then, the innocent activities of acting, painting, or writing clash with the activities of good and proper living in a well regulated society. When this happens, the artist finds himself an alien. Every connection which he makes with the organized world, in order to work or to eat, emphasizes his foreignness. Every connection comes to mean for him an adjustment and a judgment. The world judges him, but then he judges the world. James has, therefore, another vantage point for viewing the great world. He has the critique implicit in the look which the artist casts upon the spectacle spread round him.

Judgment is easy for one entirely outside the world and unattracted by it, for ivory-tower craftsmen; but James makes over and over the important point that his artist remains in the world and is enamored of it even while suffering from it in many practical ways. He exalts a sense of life with the same breath he affirms a passion for form. He fertilizes art with the vital force of living, and on the other hand, crystallizes life into enduring forms. Therefore, when James reports his artist-hero's critique of life in the well regulated society, he is reporting the perceptions of a person who loves rather than hates life. This fact makes James' treatment of the two great repulsive-attractive forces (of living and making) more central than the treatment by those who are the disgusted-with-life, upon the one hand, and those who are the disgusted-with-art, upon the other.

Since James is not a philosopher but a novelist, the treatment of the conflicts is not upon a discursive, idealized plane, but upon the embarrassed, actual level of living. Money is, for instance, a real thing for the human being who happens to be an artist, as real as his necessity to make a statue, or paint a picture, or write a book.

Ray Limbert, in the story *The Next Time,* cannot by hook or crook write anything but masterpieces. Try as he will, he fails to earn money for his family's immediate needs. While any number of writers may be embarrassed by mediocrity, Ray is embarrassed by genius. Then, as if to show how impossible it is for an artist to be right, James exhibits, in Frank Saltram, the hero of *The Coxon Fund,* a thinker and conversationalist of the Coleridge type who chokes upon a sufficiency of cash. As a fantasy upon a possible Coleridge, one assured of money and the means of living, the story illustrates the great conversational flow cut off by the very means taken to keep it going. Money again is the real thing, real enough to displace everything else.

Position, too, for the actual vain man who writes or paints, is another real thing. Vanity causes the statusless artist, drawing ideas from the pageant of the class society, to be attracted to the temptation of prestige. There is irony in James' picture of the artist, who is anything and everything in his own mind, attempting anxiously to be something or someone in the social world.

In the story *The Death of the Lion,* the great writer who has suffered himself to become the hero of the season becomes, when ill, simply an impediment to a good time. He is dying upstairs while the hostess is busied downstairs trying to smooth over this damper to her week end. It is, of course, of secondary importance to her that the sole copy of the author's as yet un-published book has been lost in the careless excitement of the party.

In *The Velvet Glove* the attraction which society exerts upon the author, John Berridge, seems snobbery. But while the story is told in terms of titles, class distinctions, and the manners of party-going noblemen, it has a meaning central to James' theme. He uses these terms to express the implacable difference between the artist's two allegiances.

As a man, John Berridge is open to flattery. He is beguiled by the marked attentions given him at a particular party by a beautiful pair of the unconscious upper classes. He almost loses his middle-aged balance under the dizzying influence of the lady until she touches upon his own writer's territory. She asks him to write a praising preface to a volume she has written, an impossible and awful book. Here the iron hand shows in his refusal.

The story is a good example of one of James' favorite contrasts, between the people who lead rich personal lives and never think, and the writer who is all reflection and who upon occasion envies the shining ones. But, pushed, he has his own pride and his own inflexibility. They, the young pair, are, in James' phrase, "Olympians," and they live "life in irreflective joy and at the highest thinkable level of prepared security and unconscious insolence," while the writer, with his eyes open to "the torment of earth," only deceives himself if he thinks he can live their splendid lives.

The tragic loss of communication is a more basic trouble of the artist than the troubles instanced above. It is a trouble which involves the reason for his existence. James treats it over and over, from many angles. In *The Author of Beltraffio* the break has occurred between the writer and the person nearest him, his wife. She thinks his good bad, and he thinks her propriety a misconceived immorality. Their delicate little boy, Dolcino, becomes the center of their struggle, which is carried to the point of the child's death.

In *The Figure in the Carpet* the loss of communication has occurred between master and disciple. Hugh Vereker sets his most astute critic upon an anguished search for meaning. He tells the young man that no critic has yet found out his plain intent, which is as obvious and visible as the pattern in the fabric of a carpet. This parable puts the break between writer and reader in the most effective and teasing form.

In addition to being misunderstood, the artist in James' tales commonly finds himself callously used by various forces of the social order. Verena Tarrant in *The Bostonians* can be taken as a key figure. With her gift of speech, she is pulled first in one direction by Olive Chancellor and then in another by Basil Ransom. Olive makes use of her for the good of humanity, and Basil, for the good of one member of humanity, himself. Since her great gift, which James presumes and persuades the reader to be genius, is lodged in a particular fallible young girl, neither she nor her gift can ever be entirely free. Verena is a real *jeune fille,* of the willful Jamesian clan, and no abstraction, yet the idea belonging to her character and situation is communicated: that art, so long as it is connected with human beings is quite likely to be either a tool of the reformer or shut away into the box of domesticity altogether.

What the artist must find is some *modus vivendi.* He must accommodate art to the condition of a human being, yet not throw it away in the adjustment. The effort is a grim one at best, as James knew in his own life. The triumphant career of his character, Miriam Rooth, in the novel *The Tragic Muse,* whom James proposes as a great actress of her time, is a continual sacrifice of one personal and human advantage after another.

A person outside the struggle might look at Miriam and her career and pronounce: "Beauty was the principle of everything she did and of the way she unerringly did it—an exquisite harmony of line and motion and attitude and tone." Yet Miriam herself could turn upon this principle of beauty and call it "the demon, the devil, the devourer, and destroyer." Reconcile the two attitudes as the observer may, the artist must effect the agreement in his own person.

William Butler Yeats' description of the artist's problem is in agreement with James when he says: "We artists suffer in our art if we do not love most of all life at peace with itself and doing without forethought what its humanity bids it and therefore happily. We are, as seen from life, an artifice, an emphasis, an uncompleted arc perhaps. Those whom it is our business to cherish and celebrate are complete arcs." And, "The arts have nothing to give but that joy of theirs which is the other side of sorrow, that exhausting contemplation. . . ."

James' positive hero, his American in Europe, his child in the corruption of society, his underprivileged boy waking to beauty, his artist in the unmanageable world, are all engaged actively in getting at the center of life. They get so far into it as to choke upon a superabundance. Another set of protagonists, his negative heroes, sicken of life's complications and turn from it to the perfect adjustment possible only upon the nonsocial and nonhuman level.

There are many stages upon the way to a complete estrangement from life. Several are told in the artist stories. One stage, described in an early story, *The Madonna of the Future,* is that of the painter who perceives the ideal of a picture of the virgin but is afraid to compromise his vision by putting it on canvas. Gabriel Nash, the art-for-art's-sake man in *The Tragic Muse,* is a witty touchstone for others, for Nick Dormer, for instance, but nothing in himself. He is an artist in attitude only. James comments severely that the artist must not only hold onto a vision of the world, he must do something with it. One loses one's innocence in the doing, but the loss is necessary since the doing, the involvement in life, is everything.

On the other hand, the picture of work done, but done in a vacuum, is a picture of futility, too. The complete and sanitary separation of art from the stain of living is described in *The Great Good Place.* This story has been described as the writer's enthusiastic vision of a dream refuge for the harassed creator. But there is an emotion of uneasiness in it, a sensation of emptiness that leads one to reconsider. George Dane's vision had come to him in an illness caused by his inability to cope with life. He had fallen away from the multiplied assault of actual living and working into a spotless dream world. The essential unhealthiness of perfect peace, segregated from the stew of life, seems to be the deepest idea in its ambiguous depths.

Another group of characters, not artists but ordinary social souls, turn away from a disappointment with life to death or the superior companionship of the dead. There is a trace of this idea in *The Birthplace* and the complete obsession with it in *The Altar of the Dead*.

Maud-Evelyn is one of James' ghost stories, but it differs from the stories mentioned above only in the degree of alienation from life which its hero suffers. He is an ineffectual young man who finds it easier to be the perfect lover of a dead girl than of a living one. The story is a curious one whose deathly chill is islanded in the tone of easy gossip.

The name, Maud-Evelyn, is that of a daughter of a wealthy couple, a girl who had died at sixteen. They have made a cult of her, gone in for communication with her by mediums, kept a part of the house set aside as her rooms, and even invented more life for her than her early death allowed her to have. They add and add to this story of what she might have done, especially after virtually adopting the penniless young man whom they begin to consider had been Maud-Evelyn's fiancé.

He who had never seen the girl enters into their life and their imaginings. He does not believe in the mediums but is impressed by the parents and to some extent their money. He is seen always from outside the household, however, and the author teases the reader with wondering how far he has gone in his connection with Maud-Evelyn. It does seem certain, however, that he has married her by the time one sees the last of him.

Each experience of stepping out of life and into another ghostly or supernatural world is a movement toward a kind of nonhuman, nonsocial perfection. The chilling spell cast upon Miles and Flora, the two children of *The Turn of the Screw,* induces a development of manner and of finish in them. They are precocious and beautiful, but hard, and with the particular horror of this story, they are children who are not just bad but are evil.

Any movement to get out of life and its rich confusion is shown over and over by James to tend to become a movement toward a sterile perfection. John Marcher in *The Beast in the Jungle* abstains from life in order to hold himself apart for a perfect action, an action which passes him by and leaves him stranded and gasping, deprived of vital breath. Ralph Pendrel in *The Sense of the Past* rejects real living in his own time and steps into an eighteenth century of his imagining. The novel, before it breaks off, begins to show Ralph as pressed and squeezed in his false role.

The dislocation from society seen in the stories mentioned above and in such others as *The Jolly Corner, The Private Life,* and *The Aspern Papers* is a part of James' theme of the individual and his relationship to society, since it is the negative inversion of that idea. The positive aspect of the theme is exhibited variously in the American in Europe, the child or young girl in society, the slums hero involved in wealth, the artist in the class order. All these observations upon American-ness, youth, poverty, and the artist's mind have reference to the one valid obsession with the individual and his social environment, the civilization made by the many, many individuals of the past.

The uninitiated hero is a person of essential freshness and individuality who attacks the citadel of society in order to enter it and complete himself. Equipped with his ardor, his sensibility, and his desires, his strangeness carries him, with the impetus of his first rush, far inside. Then, society, operating upon protective and preservative principles of its own, turns upon him, closing around him, as the amoeba surrounds the foreign particle.

James says in effect that this conflict is necessary, both for the exercise of the individual's moral and aesthetic qualities, and for the leavening of society. The individual is what he is because he has rubbed and scraped against the unamenable particles of society. He is also an irreducible self, which he continues to be in spite of the hammering, shaping strokes of society. James shows how society makes and unmakes the man, and also how, at the same time, man makes and unmakes himself. He was unable to treat one term without the other. He could not exhibit the personality simply for its consciousness. He must show the environing, influencing order surrounding that consciousness. And he could not exhibit society, in representative strata, with representative samples. He must show, in opposition and in collaboration, the vital man and the sturdy, ordered social world.

PART Four

Variations
upon the Theme

James had not so many different ideas. His stories are variations upon the theme of the individual and society outlined in the previous chapter. He used as the motive power of his narratives the basic passions of common human nature, the loves, hates, jealousies, and prides, only modified as to the form they take by the circumstance of their existing in a complex civilization.

His novels have the dimensions of breadth and depth. Although there are not so many different themes from novel to novel, within each novel James flashes at the reader many facets of the one idea. It is as if he turned the jewel of his idea from side to side so that its variety of lights shines out, one succeeding the other. And in each novel there is a depth of significance. He had the metaphorical sense to an unusual degree. In his stories one thing stands for another. There is a conscious as well as a natural and unconscious use of symbols. And there is also a suggestion of the way meaning gets into common objects and comes to stand for more than meets the eye. In the end the world of the novel seems to stand for the great world of life, with the author as the god of the small world.

One way of considering these stories is to see them as they partake of the horizontal and vertical dimensions. One can observe first the reaction of idea upon idea, character upon character, action upon action, and the flashing out of moral and aesthetic lights as the author turns the situation from side to side.

And one can then hold the jewel still and look into it and sound it for its meaning.

The previous chapter simplified James' theme for a purpose. It gave perhaps the erroneous notion that the writer's heroes exist as giants in an arena of great choices where everyone else is of pigmy size. The following discussion should place the hero in perspective. It will show him implicated in a "thick" situation and rubbing against other formidable personalities. It should restore some of the reality into the abstraction.

The unfinished novel *The Ivory Tower* is a fit illustration of James' "crooked corridor" of ideas.

The novel, whose unfinished state causes regret upon each occasion of reading it, was to break new ground. It was to show the return of the American from Europe to his native land, the return of the alien, cultured hero, to an America grown powerful and important in his absence. It was to pose the possibility of a conjunction of culture and money upon the American ground. The book's hero, Graham Fielder, was to be a new man in America and a sign for the future. How does James turn this idea from side to side before the reader? How does he cause it to excite and stimulate, as it does?

The novel, in the fragment left us, is divided into four parts. Book I is a preparation which brings on stage all the characters who are awaiting the arrival of the hero. Book II gets us inside that hero's mind as he makes his entry upon the scene. It lets us feel with him the shock of his coming immediately face to face with a situation of a size and poignancy never met before in his quiet life. Book III is the counterplotting of forceful enemies, the counterpoint of inimical desires and wills. Book IV exhibits the hero, with all his choices before him and all his dangers breathing upon him, about to act and initiate the essential drama. Then, with all the elements of the story spread in tempting array before one, the novel breaks off, in mid-sentence.

What happens is the following: Graham Fielder, innocent of business, having lived until his thirty-second year an easy-going, discriminating life in Europe, comes into an unexpected inheritance when his uncle, Mr. Betterman, dies. Rosanna Gaw, a childhood friend, has helped to make this event possible through intervention with his uncle. Horton Vint and Cissy

Foy (the enemies) form a mutual pact to assist Gray to part with his money. Cissy is to keep Gray from marrying Rosanna, and Horton is to advise Gray how to spend his fortune. Together they are to get the benefit since they are agreeably in love. At the end of the fragment, Rosanna has gone away through fear of being oppressive to Gray; Gray has made Horton his right-hand man and is about to meet Cissy.

Within this series of events are the various exciting ideas which inhabit a James story. The ideas surrounding money form a kind of circle:

a) Money can blast an individual. Rosanna's father, Abel Gaw, shown as hanging breathlessly upon the news of old Better-man's death, has been dried up by a single preoccupation with money.

b) Money can raise up beneficent, mild, and mysterious natures. Mr. Betterman is such a man. As he lies upon his deathbed, he tells Gray in cryptic language that "we require the difference that you'll make. So you see you're for our people."

c) Gray finds money a grandeur and an affront.

d) Rosanna hates each separate dollar of her millions.

e) Haughty Vint and Cissy Foy are simply greedy.

Alternating with ideas about money are those about responsibility. Rosanna has chosen twice to give a particular turn to Gray's life. She has been bold in doing so and now is afraid of what Gray will make of her. On the other hand, her father has let responsibility atrophy in him. He has surrendered entirely to the lust of gain. Gray is an unmarked card.

He has the opportunity for greatness and wonders if he has the qualities to fit him for it. He pivots between responsibility and an easier retirement into a painless, choiceless existence, a putting of himself away as he had slipped an unopened letter into the decorative case he had nicknamed "the ivory tower." Horton Vint would certainly like to make the decisions and have the trouble (and recompense) of money while Gray has only the fun.

This choice of Gray's was to have been the core of the novel. For in putting money in his nephew's hands, Mr. Betterman had placed elemental power in America back into the hands of the gentle and the sensitive. One does not know at all if Gray would have succeeded, or even if, as Cissy said, he might not have become "worse than ourselves." She agreed with Haughty Vint's description of their Newport bunch as "unspeakably corrupt."

Ideas revolving around "America" are prevalent too. The author hovers around a quiet definition of the special American quality, and questions: Is it a fine exhilaration or a flatness? America, it seems, means first of all lost bearings to Graham Fielder. Yet he turns his face upward willingly, under the Newport sky, to the "drizzle of light" of his multitudinous impressions. His opportunities are to be painful as well as magnificent in a world which is new in every respect.

The motive forces moving among these notions of Americanness, responsibility and power, are emotions and desires upon the part of each one of these difficult human beings. From the beginning these desires play one against the other. They influence action and reaction of deed and thought. Rosanna knows when she sees Gray that she has overplayed her hand. She has influenced Gray's life, but now he will have changed hers. From this moment the possessive, powerful woman is helpless, for "whatever he said or did would deprive her of resistance to an inward pressure which was growing as by the sight of him."

Upon his side, Gray was to be from the first wary, interested, open, yet holding himself off from conclusions. He swore to Vint that he would not, with wealth and position, be a façade. Yet he suffered himself to rest in Vint's persuasive care of the details and to become interested in the repeated name of Cissy Foy. And he was to find growing and growing within him the insistent desire to live up to his uncle's bequest, the difficult spiritual one, as well as the monetary one. Yet he does not know how to go about it and makes his way in the dark.

The reader sees that the forces which have been turned onto Gray are positive and strong. There will be some particular, conclusive settling of Graham Fielder before the end which one can guess but will never know. For James, although dealing in subtleties, anchors them to real and definite causes which are pushed to honest conclusions.

The instigation of such a fatal movement is perfectly seen in Gray's interview with his uncle just before the old man's death. This is a sample of the writer's ability to lift the interest out of

1e ordinary quality of living (which he has thoroughly set and
olored for one in the preceding chapter) into an emotional and
maginative reference transforming the whole story into a vision
of life as well as a report of it. Before this interview takes place,
one knows that the entire action will be a question of money.
During this chapter, it becomes clear that it is to be more: it is to
be the use of money, the imaginative understanding of its power
that is to occupy the following pages.

The mild Newport light fills the room in which Mr. Betterman lies; it seems as beneficent as he does, in his "great grave
bed." The aspect of things announces to Gray (and to the reader)
that this meeting is to be an extraordinary one.

What this chapter discloses is not just the announcement of
his inheritance, but the motive for it, which Gray only half
understands. He finds, upon stepping into the sick room, that
any easy comprehension on his part must wait upon an appraisal
of him by the dying man. And he instantly realizes that he is
upon the rack, he and his whole being.

That look which the old man gives him is a judgment such as
he has never had to meet before. And so, by transfer, he realizes
that the whole proposition of his receiving money is to be a test.
And the old man himself, whom he finds so cool and formidable
and frightening, is to be "the biggest and most native American
impression" that he could meet.

The extremes of the good of two worlds are to battle in his
mind. One is the Europe which he had chosen at fourteen in
preference to coming to America and a business education by
his uncle. The other is America as represented by the same uncle
who welcomed him now as free from a notion about business.
" 'Does it mean,' he might have murmured to himself, 'the
strangest shift of standards?' " For himself, and for Mr. Betterman, standards have indeed shifted. For to his bewilderment, the
man propped upon the pillows says: " 'My point isn't so much
for what you are as for what you're not,' " and pitilessly, " 'I've
got you—without a flaw. So!' "

So, despite himself, in the strange new light of the New World,
Gray has to face the fact of being chosen. The great strain induces the honest reply: "He stood there as for inspection, easily

awkward, pleasantly loose, holding up his head as if to make the most of no great stature. 'I've never been so sorry that there isn't more of me.' "

The two men face one another nakedly as human beings seldom do. And Mr. Betterman probes and probes for what is in Gray. Then he brings out the enlarging proposition which makes Gray, and the reader, gasp:

> "It's for the world."
> "The world?"—Gray's vagueness again reigned.
> "Well, our great public."
> "Oh your great public—!"

The exclamation, the cry of alarm, even if also of amusement in face of such a connection as that, quickened for an instant the good touch of the cool hand. "That's the way I like you to sound. It's the way she told me you *would*—I mean that would be natural to you. And it's precisely why—being the awful great public it is—we require the difference that you'll make. So you see you're for our people."

Poor Graham's eyes widened. "I shall make a difference for your people—?"

But his uncle serenely went on. "Don't think you know them yet, or what it's like over here at all. You may think so and feel you're prepared. But you don't know till you've had the whole thing up against you."

"May I ask, sir," Gray smiled, "what you're talking about?"

And later, as the light from outside grew richer, and Mr. Betterman grasped his arm, Gray heard murmured at him, in reference to the great public: " 'The enormous preponderance of money. Money is their life.' " And: " 'They're full of the poison —without a blest other idea. Now you're the blank I want.' "

So Mr. Betterman in giving, grasps him. Gray protests, yet Mr. Betterman holds him, as much by his argument as by the hand upon his arm. The old man exults with "richest gravity" to the nurse who has come to take Gray away: " 'But I've got him; I mean I make him squirm—' "

James has held the reader in the vise of interest with as much force as Mr. Betterman had held Gray by the arm. He truly makes the reader squirm for the interest and the forceful truth of such a clash of man against man. He has dived deep below the surface and into the rich levels of consciousness, "the deeper and

darker and unapparent, in which things *really* happen to us."
Yet he has taken with him, into the depths, the ability to deal with
ideas. There are here both the emotional affront dealt by one
personality to another and the intellectual shock of ideas exercised one upon the other. The best of James, as in this chapter in
an unfinished novel, brings about this union of emotional and
intellectual man.

James has not only variety and a sure grasp upon his ideas as
embodied in emotions, his novels have another dimension that
makes them original and unforgettable. This is the aforemen-
tioned depth or metaphorical sense which he possessed. It adds
the quality of the mysterious and the incalculable in a James
novel to the firm understanding which controls and guides. It is
the double-seeing power of the imagination which he had in his
own person and which he put into one or another of the characters in every story. In this novel it is the modest, accomplished
Gray, the "happy Hamlet," who sees into and beyond appearances.

There is a steady rise in the temperature of Gray's imagination from his first stepping into his new world. He is quiet and
modest, yet within begins to be master of what he perceives. He
twists and turns his situation about in order to get it into perspective. Each new American person is an experience: Mr. Gaw
and his rapacious stare, the nurses and their familiarity, his uncle
whom he recognizes as "so great a person—a presence like that of
some weary veteran of affairs," Rosanna Gaw, Haughty Vint, all
awaken his curious fancy to make out what they are and what
their alien American quality is:

> There was an American way for a room to be a room, a table a
> table, a chair a chair and a book a book—let alone a picture on a wall
> a picture, and a cold gush of water in a bath of a hot morning a
> promise of purification; and of this license all about him, in fine, he
> beheld the refreshing riot.

When Gray finds that his position in the New World is to be a
prominent one, he is not content just to enter into his new situation, he must allegorize it. He shrinks from the role of rich
man, yet his only imaginative equivalent for the position which
he is to hold is that of some kind of potentate. It seems that he,

who is so private and quiet, is to be at least a czar or a kaiser. Horton, whose relation to him already appears ambiguous, is to be his favorite; and, according to court etiquette, it seems best to keep this relationship secret from the keeper of the treasury, Mr. Crick, the flat, dry lawyer in charge of the money. And all the variegated Newport bunch revolving round him, Davey Bradham, Cissy Foy, even Rosanna Gaw, are in waiting upon him.

Gray's private speculation is not just a quaint and idle flourish round and about the truth, but an imaginative reinforcement of the truth. It is the James poetry which strikes into the mind more forcefully than bare reason could ever do.

Such imaginative speculation, too, is Gray's naming of the letter receptacle upon the piano top, the ivory case which holds shut up inside an important, unopened letter. He calls "this wonder of wasted ingenuity," which Rosanna had given to him, his "ivory tower." It is a sign of some possible future refuge that he himself might get into:

> "*Isn't* it an ivory tower, and doesn't living in an ivory tower just mean the most distinguished retirement? I don't want yet awhile to settle in one myself—though I've always thought it a thing I should like to come to."

His alternatives, the active or the passive life, have the lively and living reality of metaphors in his mind. It is to be either rule or retire. James' insight into the situation is the summarizing, concentrating power of poetry, the genius for discovering truth in memorable images. In this novel it makes one see what money is, and what responsibility means to the man who must choose power or abdicate from it.

The fragment *The Ivory Tower* indicates the two attributes, breadth and depth, which at the moment determine the method I use to appraise Henry James. By breadth, I mean variety and the imaginative understanding of human nature. By depth, I mean the special artist's metaphorical or analogical ability to see one thing stand for another.

Leaving the particular novel, I turn the method upon the whole work. First, I want to assess James' understanding of the normal and the human, and to see what light, moral, spiritual, or aesthetic, his grasp of human relations gives to a reader. As a prelude, one should underline the fact of James' appreciation of the basic passions.

The condition of James' novels being that of developed, elaborate living, too little credit has been given him for the reality of the passions shown operating in this special area. In 1894 James set down in a notebook, on October 24, the following exhortation to himself:

Plus je vais, the more intensely it comes home to me that solidity of subject, importance, emotional capacity of subject, is the only thing on which henceforth, it is of the slightest use for me to expend myself. Everything else breaks down, collapses, turns thin, turns poor, turns wretched—betrays one miserably. Only the fine, the large, the human, the natural, the fundamental, the passionate things.

In spite of minor lapses, James' unbroken career shows the strong resolve carried through with courage. It was the real things, the sincere and passionate things which occupied him and carried the weight of elaboration.

He understood that the human passions are the motive forces of life. He insisted that these passions, when described in fiction, should be real. Nothing so disgusted him as literary falsity in this connection. On Thomas Hardy's Tess he wrote to Stevenson: "But oh yes, dear Louis, she is vile. The pretence of 'sexuality' is only equalled by the absence of it." So, whether it is "sexuality" or jealousy or hate in his stories, the emotion must be sincere. Yet he was surrounded by a society (and it was the only world he knew well enough to describe) which baffled the expression of the overmastering emotions.

He turned the difficulty into an advantage. In the first place, difficulty itself stimulated him. In the second place, he understood the value of shock. The authentic feeling, arising from a background of artifice and convention, has shock value. The inevitable human passion bursts forth. The effect is a climax.

The touch of hand upon hand, Fleda Vetch's upon Owen Gereth's in *The Spoils of Poynton,* is momentous; a sudden embrace, Charlotte's and Amerigo's in *The Golden Bowl,* causes a suspension of the breath. A scene of frank seduction, such as

Julia Dallow's thwarted essay in *The Tragic Muse,* has all the advantage of knocking the props of civilized living out of the way, not only for the participant but for the reader. He has a fresh revelation: so this is the way we are!

The sensation is that of restless depths in human nature which persist in being manifested despite rules and regulations. In the novel which lives comfortably and customarily upon the physical plane, the passions become flat and stale. They are only the ordinary and acceptable biology of the human animal. In James they are in a constant, uneasy play of counterpoint with other vital elements of human nature, complicated intellectual, emotional, and aesthetic qualities which he finds real too.

In a large sense James' novels are all about one passion, the passion for life. Each one of his individual heroes is an aspirant to a larger, freer experience of living. However thwarted this or that one's desire is, one feels the warmth of the craving. It is as vital in the child, Maisie, and the adolescent, Nanda, as in the mature creatures of his imagination, Milly Theale, Lambert Strether, and Maggie Verver, each one of whom owns a whole and imaginative and conscious sense of life.

Passion, moving among the forms of society, gives one glimpses of modes above and below the crystallized forms. Yet these modes chain the passionate individual. James never lets one forget what are the conditions of life. It is as conditioned, as formed, that the big emotions appear effective, real, and touching.

Consider May Server in *The Sacred Fount,* whose love for Gilbert Long can have no open expression. Pushed by her emotion to the verge of hysteria, she can only sit and smile at the company assembled in Newmarch's spacious drawing room to listen to expensive music. She draws upon herself the consideration of the "I" of the novel, the observer who soon gets too far into the situation to be ironic: he sees pretty, distracted May Server, in her repressed fright, as

the controlling image for me, the real principle of composition, in this affluence of fine things. What, for my part, while I listened, I most made out was the beauty and the terror of conditions so highly organised that under their rule her small lonely fight with disintegration could go on without the betrayal of a gasp or a shriek.

May Server reminds him also of the frightening dependence of the individual upon the particular forms of a particular social order. Her situation emphasizes the double pressure put upon the single soul by nature and society. She reminds the storyteller, too, of what in the way of freedom that social order had missed:

We were all so fine and formal, and the ladies in particular at once so little and so much clothed, so beflounced yet so denuded, that the summer stars called to us in vain. We had ignored them in our crystal cage, among our tinkling lamps; no more free really to alight than if we had been dashing in a locked railway-train across a lovely land.

May Server is too passive to be a typical James heroine. In his major novels the terms are more evenly matched. His protagonists are full-blooded people whose desires are in a more equal proportion to the pressures of their environment. These heroes and heroines seem to represent nature as a positive force invading society and threatening the forms of society. Yet this is not all, or James would be just another common naturalist or romanticist.

In puzzling out James' placing of the individual, it is easy to oversimplify the situation. His Isabels and Hyacinths and Strethers are not just trying to get out of vexing limitations into pure freedom. They want fulfillment, they want completion, but they are looking for forms worthy of their vitality. They want forms to which they can give themselves.

Grant to James, then, the passions and the curbs. These are his constants. What his characters trace in the relationship between the two, or what some observer, part in and part out of the story, sees in the clashing and meshing of the two constants, then, are his "ideas." Since he is an artist of a special kind, he has no pure ideas. Such as they are, they are connections and interrelations.

I do not mean to say that James' ideas are not valid. I mean that they are not detachable from the story, and therefore not able to serve any other purpose than to illuminate human nature, and particular human nature, at that. His ideas have no obtrusive purpose. Like Keats' notion of great poetry, his fiction does not have "a palpable design upon us." But one can arrange a kind of circle of ideas visible as operating in the stories, one suggesting another, or its opposite, which he may cherish as well. One can begin anywhere in the discussion of his ideas, since there is no question of a system involved, perhaps with his idea of freedom.

Isabel Archer's story in *The Portrait of a Lady* is that of a search for a particular freedom. Yet with the means of gaining freedom given her in abundance, the desire for it, the necessary bravery, a flexible mind, and the money, she fails. The money enabling her to be free to choose in any matter, in marrying she chooses Gilbert Osmond as the freest man she knows. He chooses her for the money. The interesting fact about the trap into which Isabel has fallen is that she herself has been from the beginning responsible. This is true in spite of the crude deceptions practiced upon her.

Her flaw had been a desire to see yet not to feel. She had said: "It's not absolutely necessary to suffer; we were not made for that . . . that's what I came to Europe for, to be as happy as possible." Her wish was for "a full exploration of life"; her fear was of "diminished liberty." A conversation with her cousin Ralph Touchett indicates how in aiming for the one, she would achieve the other:

"You want to see life—you'll be hanged if you don't, as the young men say."

"I don't think I want to see it as the young men want to see it. But I do want to look about me."

"You want to drain the cup of experience."

"No, I don't wish to touch the cup of experience. It's a poisoned drink! I only want to see for myself."

"You want to see, but not to feel," Ralph remarked.   .

In looking around in her freedom, Isabel has given herself to the enemy. For her free man is a common snob and lover of convention. Any evasive hunt for freedom, evasive of the responsibility of feeling, fails. James thus ties responsibility to liberty.

The idea of responsibility is a personal rather than a social idea in James. One must answer for what one does. One must do and be, with all one's nature, the emotional as well as the intellectual. And freedom, with responsibility added onto freedom, means self-determination. This making out what one is is the goal of development not only for Isabel, whose hunt for freedom is the most naked, but for Roderick Hudson, artist; for Miriam Rooth, actress; Maggie Verver, wife; or Lambert Strether, ordinary human being. Each one of the restless heroes is engaged in an effort at individual self-determination. It is not a blank liberty that is sought; it is the freedom to be oneself in relation to the world.

Roderick progresses from the simple challenge of practicing law in Northampton to the complex one of making statues in Rome; Newman, from the simple challenge of making money in Wall Street to the baffling one of making a marriage in Paris; Hyacinth, from the simple duty of earning a living to the difficult one of enjoying living. Each development is accompanied by an increase of the particular, individual personality. Yet each articulation of the personality takes place in an increasingly complex social world whose pressures keep pace with the opportunities. The greater the freedom, the greater the expense.

Freedom, self-determination, responsibility, payment: these concepts have an inexorable ring in James. It is only the fact that the concepts are in solution (of art) and balanced by equally binding concepts of art that James does not suggest the moralist.

The idea of "paying for" anything that a person gets in life pervades all his stories, as the idea did his own life. In *The Middle Years,* the broken narrative of his experience of Europe, James measured in his own life the relationship of pain and paying to the gaining and enjoying, for

the authenticity of whatever one was going to learn in the world would probably always have for its sign that one got it at some personal cost. To this generalisation mightn't one even add that in proportion as the cost was great, or became fairly excruciating, the lesson, the value acquired would probably be a thing to treasure? I remember really going so far as to wonder if any act of acquisition of the life-loving life-searching sort that most appealed to me wouldn't mostly be fallacious if unaccompanied by that tag of the price paid in personal discomfort, in some self-exposure and some none too impossible consequent discomfiture for the sake of it.

The drift of the argument suggests Emerson without optimism; only the bad compensates for the good, rather than the good for the bad.

Another originality in James' thought is that it is particularly the good thing for which one pays rather than the bad thing. Since the consciousness of life is the greatest thing, there the expense is the greatest. Milly Theale's payment with death for life is deliberate and knowing rather than mercifully unconscious. It is a transaction between living and dying agreed upon, signed, sealed, and delivered in a particular meditation. She determines, upon learning the short term of life left her (a verdict having been pronounced upon her by a great doctor): "Since I've lived all these years as if I were dead, I shall die, no doubt as if I were alive."

She has reached this new solitude, away from everyone she knows, and sits upon a park bench considering not only herself, but in the light of death, the poorly clothed, lonely park frequenters round her:

> The real thing was to be quite away from the pompous roads, well within the centre and on the stretches of shabby grass. Here were benches and smutty sheep; here were idle lads at games of ball, with their cries mild in the thick air; here were wanderers, anxious and tired like herself; here doubtless were hundreds of others just in the same box. Their box, their great common anxiety, what was it, in this grim breathing-space, but the practical question of life? . . . All she thus shared with them made her wish to sit in their company.

What the doctor had let her know had stripped her of superfluities of material furnishings:

> Its operation for herself was as directly divesting, denuding, exposing. It reduced her to her ultimate state, which was that of a poor girl—with her rent to pay for example—staring before her in a great city. Milly had her rent to pay, her rent for the future; everything else but how to meet it fell away from her in pieces, in tatters. . . . She looked about her again . . . at her scattered, melancholy comrades—some of them so melancholy as to be down on their stomachs in the grass, turned away, ignoring, burrowing.

Milly learns, as Isabel does, as Lambert Strether does, the value which living can take on for the expanded imagination. That imagination, stretched and pulled to its limits, betrays her as it rewards. The same quality had shown her creator, too, how "there plays inveterately within the beautiful, if it but go far enough, the fine strain of the tragic."

Another potent example is Maggie Verver in *The Golden*

Bowl. She expands to good fortune, the fortune of husband and home and child, in humble gratitude, confessing that it has always been her way to "tremble for her life." Yet when the marriage turns bad, it is Maggie who shifts the burden of paying upon herself. This law in James has its supreme exhibit in Maggie's case: the injured one, the good one, pays and expiates, not for the wrong she has done, but for the wrong which has been done her.

One strange revelation of these novels is that goodness may provoke evil. By being conspicuous enough, proud enough, or blind enough it does just that. Maggie's eyes had been closed to evil as if it had not existed. She had never had anything bad happen to her. So, in making it easy for herself to be deceived, she had helped in her own betrayal. She pays for not understanding about evil. What she then has to absorb and make part of her is the daily, intimate pressure of it, "the horror of finding evil seated all at its ease where she had only dreamed good."

Maggie begins to live when she begins to know pain. One muses upon the fact that Maggie's sin, if one can impute sin to her, is the unwillingness to acknowledge pain and badness. Her fault is reminiscent of Isabel, who wanted to see but not to feel, and of Roderick, who had imaginative brilliance without common sympathy. When they begin to pay in their own flesh and in their own imagination, they then live.

A great deal of the power of James' stories lies in his quiet assumption of people's willingness to take advantage of each other, to look upon the others not as valuable individuals, but as things to be used. This is the unforgivable sin in the author's lexicon. The concept goes back with directness and purity to the father's teachings. The elder Henry James put the idea thus, in a letter to Caroline Tappan:

No human being can afford to commit his happiness to another's keeping, or, what is the same thing, forego his own individuality with all that it imports. The first requisite of our true relationship to each other (spiritually speaking) is that we be wholly independent of each other: then we may give ourselves away as much as we please, we shall do neither them nor ourselves any harm. But until that blessed day comes, by the advance of a scientific society among men, we shall be utterly unworthy to love each other or be loved in return. We shall do nothing but prey upon each other and turn each other's life to perfect weariness.

Rejecting his father's urgent hope of the perfectibility of man, the younger Henry James acknowledged the negative side of this truth operating in mortal combinations available for his fiction. The provocation of the bad is in part the beautiful, unconscious insolence of goodness. Yet the prime impulse to use the other person seems to have a native sufficiency. It exists and works and is not just made by circumstances: evil is a fundamental condition of human nature in James' fiction. The face which it puts on for him is the use made of one person by another.

In *The American,* Christopher Newman is in some way badly used by the De Cintrés. In the previous novel Roderick Hudson had been betrayed by Christina Light. Yet the fall of these early heroes is swathed in a kind of grand vagueness. James' grasp of causes and effects became more evident as he came to specify and objectify the motives of his characters. A part of his growth was in this process.

It is the "grasping imagination," which James assumed he had, that can introduce the ugly real into a novel and yet attain with that novel a leading impression of the beautiful. This he did in *The Wings of the Dove, The Ambassadors,* and *The Golden Bowl.* They are his greatest novels. In them he has the flexibility to cope with complex truth. A great part of this grasp, which makes the bad part and parcel of the good, is the ability to delineate motives.

The fact that he shows Kate Croy's restrictive background in *The Wings of the Dove* makes one able to understand her. The poverty, the uncertainty, the dishonor of her father's house determine her course of action after she meets Milly Theale. Her use of Milly, while not forgiven nor explained away by her previous environment, is understood. The long introduction to the main situation is a prelude which serves to place Kate for the reader. Her actions thereafter, in a very different world, constitute a reference to the ugly room in which she first appears.

The leading impression of *The Ambassadors* is the loveliness of Paris and Strether's yielding to that loveliness. Yet the grotesque commonness of the Pococks, Sarah and Jim and Mamie, is needed to show why Strether, given his imagination, would turn from the Pococks' world to the other. Paris without the Pococks would lose half its charm. The strange, late poetry of Strether's falling in love with life (at fifty-five) carries all the rest with it. But swimming along in the wake of this impression are the Pococks, genuine, limited, and intense. There is not a bigger attainment in James than this mixture of the ordinary, the mediocre, and the grand. The grand does not suffer but gains by the contrast.

In *The Golden Bowl,* James does full justice to Charlotte's and the Prince's romance. He even gives it the justice of a certain amount of poetry. One knows it to be a long-lived, thwarted, true relationship. Then its continuance, by reason of its genuineness, works to the detriment of the two innocents: Maggie, the Prince's wife; Adam, Charlotte's husband. It is only by giving the old emotion its full due that James throws into proper perspective its malignity of purpose in a new situation.

When James shows one person making use of another, as indicated above, or elsewhere (Mrs. Gereth using Fleda in *The Spoils of Poynton,* Mrs. Brook using her own daughter in *The Awkward Age,* the stepparents using Maisie in *What Maisie Knew*), he exacts the price of a strong emotional response for right understanding. But he does so fairly. All the reasons are there, however disguised by human subterfuge. He does not explain; the actions explain.

What holds James' "ideas," freedom, responsibility, paying, exploiting, and so forth, in union is the aesthetic sense. After all the talk of exploitation and payment, it is time to remember that James was a novelist, not a moralist. His ideas do not become that "truth carried out to the bitter end" which Kierkegaard described. His ideas are carried out only so far as not to destroy the shape of the novel or story which contains them. They are spokes to hold the wheel to its roundness. He was not a scientist, as the naturalists thought themselves, a philosopher, or a propagandist. He was the artist guided by the artist's sense of life.

That sense of life (the joy of life added to the rectitude of life) is the light which guided not only the writer, but, inside the novels, instigated and initiated his heroes into an expansion of the soul. For his heroes are all artists to a certain extent. They come to be like Valentin de Bellegarde in *The American,* whose quick play of mind "assured you he was not economising his consciousness, not living in a corner of it to spare the furniture of the rest. He was squarely encamped in the centre and was keeping open house. When he flared into gaiety it was the movement of a hand that in emptying a cup turns it upside down."

All of them, Roderick, Newman, Isabel, Hyacinth, Maggie, Milly, and Strether, are artists in sensibility if not in profession. They all have a piece of Henry James in them. They react against arbitrary rules, "Keep off the grass" signs as their creator did. They desire to find out for themselves; they dare to cross boundaries and go over into unexplored territory. They build, they synthesize a personal, coherent world out of a profusion of riches. Of course, to the artist, the mixture of good and bad is riches.

Their geographical and social movements are no more than the outward expression of the inner desire to be like Valentin and encamp in the center of their consciousness. To give that center of themselves more room, they go from the "thin" to the "thick." It is spiritual generosity. Like Roderick Hudson, they "can't always be arranging grand bargains."

So much for the horizontal dimension, the rational grasp of human relations. Now for the vertical dimension, the nonrational and intuitional grasp of life.

One arrives at this element in James only by a roundabout trip through the man's work. One is affronted first by the fact that he is a worldly author. He is, in fact, the most mundane of writers. He speaks in *The Middle Years* of "my fate. This doom of inordinate exposure to appearances, aspects, images, every protrusive item almost, in the great beheld sum of things." But, then, what he sees in this stubborn reality and what he makes of it constitute his force.

The connecting link between object and author is the subjective imagination. Whatever he beheld, however great or trivial, in order to become material for building fiction, had to be worked upon by that power. In fact, no person and no object were of the slightest use to him until they had been so worked and shaped by the imagination. The book, when completed and separated from himself, became then another "thing," with a passion and life of its own.

In the light of the subjective imagination, "appearances, aspects, images" take on a significance to which most men are blind. It is this insight which pours energy into the modes he invented.

First, one should admit freely that this imagination had an abnormal growth in James. Its exercise in the dilemmas of everyday living often had a comic look. It seemed awkward, elaborate, or fantastic. Even his extraordinary conversation seems to have had its element of absurdity. But when the writer turned this powerful eye of the imagination upon its proper field, what he named as "the fine, the large, the human, the natural, the fundamental, the passionate things," then it operated with perfect justice. There, in a world worthy of it, it became a liberalizing, enlarging, and enriching force.

James' growth lay in his control over a greater and greater complication of significance. It was a significance particularly tied to objective appearances. He held fast to subject and plot and dramatic interest, that is, to the basic narrative pull which makes the reader want to know what is going to happen next; and added to this structure layer upon layer of meaning. In his novels, and most markedly in the later ones, all objects, all persons shine with this excess of significance. It is truth immanent, truth in things.

The source of James' insight is nonrational. However well he manipulated the fruits of this insight, its source was intuitional. It is difficult to put one's finger on method in intuition. The results are so many-sided, so varied, so all-pervasive: the quality sought is more an attitude toward material than a specific use of it. The material is the world, the persons, the places, the things which presented themselves to his senses. Some of the nameable means used to translate for the reader what his imagination saw in these things are: image, metaphor, simile, symbol, and analogy.

The manner of working might at first sight seem only a matter of words. His pages flash and shine with figures of speech. They are often poetic, of a larger reference than the immediate context, and they serve to widen boundaries of meaning. Occasionally the enlarging image is set side by side with the humorous or the merely flat and accurate observation of human nature. (As when Mrs. Gedge in *The Birthplace* says, " 'We shall live as in a fairy tale,' and picks a fly out of the butter!") The device gives an ironic flavor to his pages. But it is more than a matter of words. One remembers the resonance of certain actions and certain scenes: the translation of insight into fiction is as much a matter of situation as of word. But one sees the connection. He uses situations as if they were figures of speech. They flash a condensed meaning backward or forward along the pages of the story. Finally, in the largest sense, one comes to see the novel itself as an image or symbol.

Face the difficulty of the entire manner. Complication of insight causes complication of manner. The difficulty of his later novels and tales is due just to this excess of meaning which he discerned in the sensuous reality of the universe. He attempted with a worthy heroism to cram that excess of meaning into fiction: he was competent to do so. That is why we read him.

One can by rude analysis break down what is all of a piece in the stories and see what parts there are that go to make up James' vertical dimension.

To begin with the simpler mysteries, there is the naming of things. Since the least part of his stories partakes of the quality of the whole, even the titles are particular references. At first, the titles were sound and honest descriptions: *The American, The Europeans, Washington Square, The Portrait of a Lady,* and *The Bostonians;* as he developed, the titles turned into metaphors containing the whole meaning of the story: *The Spoils of Poynton, The Sacred Fount, The Wings of the Dove, The Ambassadors, The Golden Bowl,* and *The Ivory Tower.*

Within the story itself, names suggest the bodies to which they are fastened. Never as assiduous as some of the earlier novelists in the literal description of characters or places by name, yet James satisfies by fitness and suggestiveness. Consider Mr. Mudge, the grocer; Mrs. Bread, the nurse; and Hyacinth Robinson's fellow workers in the bookbindery, Grugan, Roker, and Hotchkin. Consider Hyacinth Robinson, himself, his name proclaiming a nature looking two ways. Consider a selection of the names of country houses scattered throughout the works: Summersoft and Gardencourt, Catchmore, Mundham, Longlands of Lady Demesne, Pasterns of the Cantervilles, Matcham, and Prestidge.

While the consonance between name and personality is not always obvious, in many cases consideration will show an appeal at least to the unconscious. It is not too farfetched to suggest that the name of Mark Ambient, who is the "author of *Beltraffio*," carries in it the two counter but necessary qualities of a writer, or that Olive Chancellor's last name underlines her directorial qualities, or that Isabel Archer's suggests the trajectory of her aspiring individuality.

The naming of persons and places leads one to consider the significance that James saw as residing in the actual persons and places. Two ways of looking at this obsession are proper: one, that actual objects had a predominant power over his imagination; the other, the fact that he saw in the object a virtue which surpassed even though it could not be separated from the object itself.

Ralph Pendrel in *The Sense of the Past* had written:

"There are particular places where things have happened, places enclosed and ordered and subject to the continuity of life mostly, that seem to put us into communication, and the spell is sometimes made to work by the imposition of hands, if it be patient enough, on an old object or an old surface."

Ralph tests his theory on his own nerves in an old house he has inherited in London. When he walks through the door of Number 9, Mansfield Square, he walks out of the smells, the sounds, and sights of the twentieth century into those of the house's past. His scholar's "sense of the past" has become the present and enclosed him. From being a passive student of that time, he becomes an actor in it. It is the house itself, the physical structure, which has accomplished the wonder. Its appropriate pictures and chairs and tables, its proportioned doorways and windows, its polished floors, are the agents of the spell.

In another old house, upon a "jolly corner" near Washington Square, Spencer Brydon tracks an apparition through empty rooms and up and down great staircases. Not jolly at all, this old family house acts upon him to show him another self that he might have been. The "thing," which begins to tire of being hunted, soon turns to follow him. Again, it is the place which has invoked the crisis and determined the form his spiritual

malaise should take, that of hunting down a specter of himself
in a house in which he might have lived.

"Europe," a continent wrought into a symbol by the subjective imagination, becomes the archetype of James' obsession
with place. It is a house through whose bewildering halls wanders a succession of strangers. The significance of place in the
idea of "Europe" is highly worked and artificial, in the best
sense of the word. It is geography not lost but contained in the
symbol.

In *The Ambassadors* the sense of Europe, growing in Lambert Strether, finds concentrated expression in a place, Paris, and
in a person, Chad Newsome. The particular sight of Chad in
an opera box accomplishes the fusion: not Paris alone, but Paris
in Chad, becomes his idea of what his life might have been. Yet
Chad lives as a particular person, a brutal young man who is
yet splendid, finished, polished, educated enough by living to
dazzle the more humane, older man. Chad in his rich setting
catches Strether's essential imagination and the total impression works to change him into a new Lambert Strether. That
new self comes to reject Chad, but it was nevertheless made by
him.

There are other places and other persons of the same double
intensity: Poynton, the house that divides mother and son; Roderick, a classic type of the romantic artist as Hugh Dencombe
is the classic type of the unromantic artist; Miriam Rooth, an
actress and also *the* actress; Verena Tarrant, who is a likable,
ignorant girl, and who also stands for art.

But look around inside the stories, where the slightest touches
tell. Aside from locations and characters, things, real and touch-
able objects, take on an unforced life by reference to a larger
meaning.

Such a detail as the eyeshade in *The Aspern Papers*, never
explained, only described as there, hiding the "divine Juliana's" eyes, creates an impression out of proportion to the intrinsic importance of the object. The relation of the prosaic
green eyeshade to the idea of the story is never stated. In fact, the
theme as such is not elaborated. But the conjunction of the action
and the emblem acts to convey the idea straight into the imagination of the reader.

This strange story is an amalgam of opposites: it has an element of the detective thriller in it, yet its atmosphere is evocative and reflective, while its subject matter is the thorny intellectual problem of the comparative rights of privacy and criticism. The hero's intrusion into Miss Bordereau's house (to gain access to a dead poet's letters to her) has its most telling moment in connection with the eyeshade. The old woman confronts the young man rifling her room, putting hands upon her secrets. Here is the way James conveys the sense of violation:

Juliana stood there in her nightdress, by the doorway of her room, watching me; her hands raised, she had lifted the everlasting curtain that covered half her face, and for the first, the last, the only time I beheld her extraordinary eyes. They glared at me; they were like the sudden drench, for a caught burglar, of a flood of gaslight; they made me horribly ashamed. I never shall forget her strange little bent white tottering figure, with its lifted head, her attitude, her expression; neither shall I forget the tone in which as I turned, looking at her, she hissed out passionately, furiously:
"Ah you publishing scoundrel!"

The homely eyeshade thus plays its part in the climax.

Pictures upon the wall in three novels have a certain resounding importance. First, in *The Wings of the Dove* the Bronzino which hangs in the gallery at Matcham serves to show Milly Theale, whom it resembles, what it is to be fixed, young and dead, forever. Then, the portrait in *The Sense of the Past* of a dead gentleman of 1820 seems to Ralph Pendrel, looking at it in the empty house of his ancestors, to have a secret meaning about that past he loves. The fact that the young man of the picture averts his face arouses an interest which is more of a sickness than a curiosity. Upon the night of wind, rain, and bluster when Ralph discovers that the young man has turned round and is looking at him, he marks the stupendous fact that the past is now accessible to him. Third, in *The Sacred Fount* there is a sort of double allegory, the entire story being one, and the episode of the picture of the Man with the Mask in his Hand being an intensification of the theme:

"Don't we want," I asked of Mrs. Server, "to know what it means?"
The figure represented is a young man in black—a quaint, tight black dress, fashioned in years long past; with a pale, lean, livid face

and a stare, from eyes without eyebrows, like that of some whitened old-world clown. In his hand he holds an object that strikes the spectator at first as some obscure, some ambiguous work of art, but that on a second view becomes a representation of a human face, modelled and coloured, in wax, in enamelled metal, in some substance not human. The object thus appears a complete mask, such as might have been fantastically fitted and worn.

The face of the man is ugly while the mask is that of a beautiful, smiling woman. As noted before, *The Sacred Fount* is a fable about a man's appropriation of his mistress' wit and brilliance as she fades and disintegrates. The appropriateness of the picture is apparent. Although the symbolism is more highly worked than is customary in James, it is in keeping with the particular novel.

Usually his use of objects as symbols is easy and natural. The things have a necessary part to play in the common-sense line of action, and the larger significance he causes one to see as belonging to them seems a legitimate addition to some ordinary use. The letter container in *The Ivory Tower,* the "tower" of the novel, is a case in point. The actual physical object is not so impressive, but the play of words and thoughts exercised upon it gain it a meaning for Rosanna and Gray which is taken over by the reader.

Similarly, the aptness of the "golden bowl" of the novel of that name—a cracked crystal covered with an expensive plating—to stand for Maggie's marriage is not forced. James places it for the reader in its actuality at the beginning when Charlotte's and the Prince's conversation over its possibility as a wedding present from Charlotte to Maggie reveals the relationship of the two, Maggie's fiancé and Maggie's friend.

Then one loses sight of the bowl. The story takes its course propelled by character and action. The sudden reappearance of the bowl in the climactic center of the story has a legitimate excitement. There is an element of chance in Maggie's discovery of it (after all, not chosen by Charlotte as appropriate), but James risks the use of chance so long as chance works as a proper element. The bowl acts as a forcing agent upon Maggie's imagination. She had known but not entirely acknowledged the truth of her husband's infidelity. The incident of the bowl (and the gossip concerning those who previously asked about it, related to her by the shopkeeper) precipitates her comprehension. Her action is a deliberate use of the object to invoke a crisis. She places it on display so that the Prince will have to come upon it. The novel gains point and poignancy by this economy of action.

In his preface to *The Golden Bowl* James shows his awareness of the extraordinary quality which this novel, as well as the other later ones, had taken on just by the development of the method and manner here noted:

We talk here, naturally, not of non-poetic forms, but of those whose highest bid is addressed to the imagination, to the spiritual and the aesthetic vision, the mind led captive by a charm and a spell, and incalculable art.

In this sphere there can be no "senseless separations," as he says in the same preface: for rich situations, there are rich and generous words. For it is by means of a particular use of words, by metaphors and similes, that James pins down elaborate thought to the sensuous real. The more complicated the state of mind, the more objective the image used to convey it swiftly to the reader.

Psychological analysis can be used to spin out motives to an abstract thinness lost to all warmth. In his mature novels James circumvents this thinness by his figures of speech. One figure after another flows out of the contemplation of action and character. Stroke by stroke the psychological is allied to the sensuous. Again one may say: This is James' slavery to the object, or: This is his freedom to see life in the object.

The habit of the writer's mind was an inveterate one. He spoke once of Emerson in an essay in *Partial Portraits* as, "Mercury, shivering in a mackintosh, bearing nectar and ambrosia to the gods whom he wished those who lived in cabins to endeavor that they might be." And in *The American Scene* occurred his memorable treatment of physical New York, "the huge jagged city,"

jagged, in her long leanness, where she lies looking at the sky in the manner of some colossal hair-comb turned upward and so deprived of half its teeth that others, at their uneven intervals, count doubly as sharp spikes.

The gift, developed elaborately in his later fiction, as every gift he had was so developed, appears there as a constructive tool. It has an intrinsic place in the story and, however colorful, is not just decorative. In illustration, one sees how in two instances, in *The Sacred Fount* and in *The Spoils of Poynton,* he illuminates the extreme of passion. The imagery employed in his figures not only describes the emotion but translates it for quick understanding. And beyond this, the force of the picture foretells the power of the emotion to act. Thus the image is a sort of prophecy of the future of the story.

Of May Server, in *The Sacred Fount,* her narrator says:

> I saw as I had never seen before what consuming passion can make of the marked mortal on whom with fixed beak and claws, it has settled as on a prey. She reminded me of a sponge wrung dry and with fine pores agape. Voided and scraped of everything, her shell was merely crushable.

Of Fleda Vetch, in *The Spoils of Poynton,* the storyteller remarks that her secret motive

> was like some dangerous, lovely living thing that she had caught and could keep—keep vivid and helpless in the cage of her own passion and look at and talk to all day long.

Yet the image has a wider use. It does more than make vivid states of mind. It lights up entire situations. It saves explanation by transcending explanation. In *The Golden Bowl* Maggie Verver's unanalyzed inner trouble becomes to her

> some wonderful beautiful but outlandish pagoda, a structure plated with hard bright porcelain, coloured and figured and adorned at the overhanging eaves with silver bells that tinkled ever so charmingly when stirred by chance airs. She had walked round and round—that was what she felt; she had carried on her existence in the space left her for circulation, a space that sometimes seemed ample and sometimes narrow: looking up all the while at the fair structure that spread itself so amply and rose so high, but never quite making out as yet where she might have entered had she wished.

And later, when Maggie perceives that the erring wife, Charlotte, has been claimed in effective silence by the husband, Adam, and that Charlotte acquiesces; she sees the two of them and their connection in the form of a picture, as if "he had been thought of as holding in one of his pocketed hands the end of a long silken halter looped round her beautiful neck."

And to go on by way of illustration, although it may seem strange in *The Wings of the Dove* to compare Milly Theale, who is all spontaneous youth and desire, to a Byzantine princess; it is in the suggestion of the fixity and angularity of that mode that the reader begins to see how bound Milly is, how caught, placed, and patterned by illness and death, and how beautiful.

The method is a dangerous one for the irresponsible. But James was never distracted by his facility into piling image upon image simply because he was able to do so. Instead of a free play of mind, he kept a firm hold upon the story line and introduced the imagery into that story as an effective element of development. The figure of speech affects the action as well as provides reflection upon it. Its force moves the reflecting character onto a further stage. Thought thus acts.

Meaning is condensed into the names of things, into common household objects, and particularly into figures of speech. Now, look at meaning packed into certain actions or happenings. Instead of a figure of speech, take, as an instance, an actual limited occurrence. One can see how it serves as a unit in the manner of a metaphor. It lights the past and foretells the future. It is the extreme example of James' compulsion to objectify. He prefers to demonstrate by action rather than explain by rational discussion.

For example, the sight of Chad Newsome entering an opera box in formal dress has a disproportionate effect upon Lambert Strether in *The Ambassadors*. The commonplace business of the opera box constitutes thereafter a private point of reference for Strether. It marks the initiation of his imagination into a new world. Another scene which also involves Chad marks a graver moment of his development. For the simple sight of Chad and his mistress, Marie de Vionnet, in a boat, upon a pretty stretch of river, marks the entrance of a long deferred judgment into Strether's new world of reactions. It marks his realization that penalities are involved in the state of life so well exemplified by the fortunate Chad. The fact that James uses certain devices to prolong such a scene and to throw it into an unnatural largeness belongs to a discussion of his style. The fact to be noted here is that he is successful in his method, that all the meaning that he could wish inheres in the scene and convinces without argument.

Now observe the process at work in *The Wings of the Dove*. Before the action proper begins, the author places his heroine upon a perilous seat upon a Swiss mountaintop and lets her survey her future. That is what, by inference, the reader assumes that she is doing there, for one does not know her thoughts.

The *mise en scène* is suggestive enough: "The girl's seat was a slab of rock at the end of a short promontory or excrescence that merely pointed off to the right into gulfs of air." Her attitude is that of one faced with an immediate alternative. Her act of refusing the final one of suicide decides her fate. Everything in her story follows logically from that scene. There is very little verbalization of the choice. James trusted his visual sense, which he possessed to an extreme, to make clear the proposition by demonstration.

This kind of scene, coming as it does customarily in his novels at widely spaced intervals, gives the reader a breathing space, an instant in which to gather together loose threads and to form an intuition of the whole. It is unanalyzed but convincing truth. Such another scene, much later than the mountaintop scene, in the same novel, is Milly's confrontation of the picture which resembles her, the Bronzino, which hangs in one of the rich rooms at Matcham, where she attains the peak of her success as a rarity of the season. On the mountaintop in Switzerland she had resolved to live. For months she had savored the experience. The Bronzino shocks her into remembrance. After all, it says, there is to be a limit:

She found herself, for the first moment, looking at the mysterious portrait through tears . . . the face of a young woman, all magnificently drawn, down to the hands, and magnificently dressed; a face almost livid in hue, yet handsome in sadness and crowned with a mass of hair rolled back and high, that must, before fading with time, have had a family resemblance to her own. The lady in question, at all events, with her slightly Michaelangelesque squareness, her eyes of other days, her full lips, her long neck, her recorded jewels, her brocaded and wasted reds, was a very great personage—only unaccompanied by joy. And she was dead, dead, dead. Milly recognized her exactly in words that had nothing to do with her. "I shall never be better than this."

Here is a portent to which she must listen and whose language she understands. And Milly lives her moment and laughs: " 'Of course her complexion's green . . . but mine's several shades greener.' " James never forgot that Milly, or any other of his characters was a person; not just a stick to stand for youth or beauty. James is portentous but he always keeps the authentic tone of the character involved, and the impressive moments in which the character is identified with some universal attribute fit into the kind of thing which would happen to such a person. Milly may know that she is to die, but she is still Milly, and anything her mind touches involves her wit. The action moves on without becoming lumpish or stuffy.

In the story *The Author of Beltraffio*, Mark Ambient's first words about his wife tell more than he should to a stranger about his marriage, but the scene has only the normal atmosphere of embarrassment following upon a break in etiquette. He says: " 'Ah, there she is! . . . and she has got the boy.' " Its symbolism is not particularly emphasized. But the reader remembers the words when the struggle between husband and wife over the child succeeds in killing him. It is like James to go thus from the conversational to the shriek by imperceptible stages.

The previous discussion has pointed to certain devices James used to gain richness of meaning. What amounts to a larger factor entirely is an element not easily isolated. This is what may be called the legendary or fairy-tale aspect, a shadowy entity existing within the novel and yet not entirely contained therein. It is as if the story, whose joyful or painful windings one follows through its characters' real world, exists on another level, too, and is told in another language.

The fairy-tale version of the story is not the dominant one. But it has an important function. It exists as a reference or as an analogy to the complex, earthbound, evil-dominated primary version. It acts as a commentary upon it. It indicates the emotional tone of the complex structure. It points and concentrates the reader's attitude. It focuses emotion.

If the reader, making his way through the difficult involvement of the novel, has in the back of his mind this easier version (which is yet in agreement with the more complex one), he makes his way through symbol and extended metaphor with greater ease and with a greater relish for the fitness, one to the other, of the various parts of the elaborate whole. If he once sees that nearly any novel of the writer might begin "Once upon a time" and be concentrated with a succinct and naïve distinctness into a paragraph, then he is free of the whole jungle of growth before him. He has the clue in his hand.

The figures of speech then knock out windows in the wall between the apparent and the unapparent. They have a double use: they tie the story to the sensuous real and at the same instant point beyond that reality to a more inclusive aspect of things. "Aspects" in James are deceptive: they are those "aspects which, under a certain turn of them, may be all but everything; gathered together they become a symbol of what is behind." The imagery, the symbolism, the situations used as figures, all can be seen as links between the primary version of the story and the secondary, the fairy-tale version.

The legendary side of Milly Theale's story, in which she is a princess, a dove whose wings finally cover everything; or of Strether's story, in which he goes upon his curious embassage; or of Hyacinth Robinson's, in which he is the traditional apprentice in love with the lady; or of Isabel's and her four suitors is simply that reality which appearances sometimes hide and sometimes reveal. It is what is beyond the wall of the average and the ordinary.

To summarize, the reader with the clue finds that James' fiction is in the main tied to the earth by the words and deeds of his characters. But it is just as evident that this sympathy for the appearances of things did not inhibit him. In the earthbound objects (persons, places, things) he uncovered reverberant meanings.

The final impression made upon the attentive reader is that the novel too is a "thing." The book itself, the finished product, the story printed upon a certain number of pages bound between two covers, is a kind of object. It is a small and complete world within the great world. And the fabricator, who is the god of this special world, stands responsible for the work he has done.

PART Five

Attitudes

THE CREATIVE ARTIST MARKS OFF THE BOUNDARY BETWEEN the unknowable and the known, between the uncontrollable and the controlled, between the flux and the form. He owes his conscience the duty to make and to shape, but with his superior equipment for receiving impressions, he knows how infinitely much more there is to be known, to be controlled, to be formed than is obvious to the childish perceptive equipment of the average man. The finished piece of work he knows to his despair is only a token of what might be done.

In considering an artist as a conscious worker, one should note first his relations to the unknown and note his bearing at the shadowy gateway where the conscious and the unconscious meet, where ideas come into being, that point at which he makes the utmost reach of his mind.

What might have wrecked a smaller mind was James' strength, a constant racking of his being by two instincts: one, to encompass all the sinuous, lengthening possibilities of a subject, pursuing it to its subtlest reaches and filling in and enriching the entire living stretch of ground covered; and two, by as powerful an impulse, to cut off, delimit, shape, perfect, and make definite that same stretch of the imagination.

His work became more difficult with his years of experience, because he saw more in a subject to be encompassed as his consciousness grew adept and supple. The other side of his mind was less and less pleased with the sloppiness of mere aspiration.

The thing had to be done, not just desired. So the work became more difficult, the struggle harder as each succeeding piece rounded into a larger ambition of the unsatisfied mind.

James said once that relations end nowhere, that the art of writing fiction (or of painting a portrait, making a statue, erecting a cathedral) consists in the laying down over the web of living relationships a circle which puts an arbitrary limit just at a certain point; just here, or there, and nowhere else. The vibration of his being between the two extremes, of the endlessness of things to be known and the definiteness of things to be done, exercised him and refined him as an artist, and as a man wearied him all his long lifetime of work. Yet it is in this awareness of the extremes of art, its two faces, that his work has vitality, even in its excesses.

He was shy of talking about inspiration. He spoke with an offhanded casualness of ideas whisking by, which, in passing, he, as a fortunate fisherman, caught just by the tips of their tails. In his prefaces he recreates the initial situation and reveals himself in an attitude of catching at these notions, pulling them out of that living but shapeless sea of energy, knocking off the excrescences hanging to them, and then setting to work with the full force of his conscious mind to make of them what he could.

The artist, as James understood him, must have great dexterity. He must be able to make a complete turnabout of attitude, not once, but over and over. He must be able to be passive and active by turns in endless and unmarked repetitions for the life of his work. For one to whom control was a sacred necessity, laxness, strange to say, was just as necessary. The ability to refuse to control must come to him as easily as the opposite impulse. The vague and wandering habits of the easy-going schoolboy, who leaned his head against iron railings to watch cows munching dreamily upon the enclosed grass, must be held onto and turned loose upon command.

James never had the presumption to forget the mystery of beginnings. And he knew that to be responsible in the end, the artist must be irresponsible at first. He speaks of the source of ideas as a "deep well" and as a "reservoir." In the preface to *The American* he says enough about the germ idea of that novel to show his entire respect for the uncontrolled initiation of themes. Here is the manner in which he speaks:

> I was charmed with my idea, which would take, however, much working out; and precisely because it had so much to give, I think, must I have dropped it for the time into the deep well of unconscious cerebration: not without the hope, doubtless, that it might eventually emerge from that reservoir, as one had already known the buried treasure to come to light, with a firm iridescent surface and a notable increase of weight.

And of the character of Christopher Newman, his arch-American, he says:

> I have, I confess, no memory of a disturbing doubt; once the man himself was imaged to me (and *that* germination is a process almost always untraceable) he must have walked into the situation as by taking a pass-key from his pocket.

He will not take credit where credit is not due. He must simply lay himself open to impressions, for he does not know what careless sight or sound may become important. James had the good sense not to be particular where he got his ideas. In a certain sense an artist cannot afford to be fastidious. He picks up his ideas as they come to him, out of the rubbish heap or out of the mouths of the uncreative. For, once he has hold of the idea, then that relentless, ever moving imagination, working for the most part in the dark, will transform it. It is only the first moment of contact that is entirely unpredictable. Therefore the artist must maintain access, be open, be unarmed.

Keats' relation to the world of the senses, the intense awareness which he had of other presences, was similar to James'. His description of that awareness is like an expansion of James' own phrase, "the fiery furnace of people." This is Keats:

> When I am in a room with People if I ever am free from speculating on creations of my own brain, then not myself goes home to myself: but the identity of every one in the room begins to press upon me that I am in a very little time an[ni]hilated—not only among Men; it would be the same in a Nursery of children.

In his Prefaces, James traces some of his ideas back to their initiation in the beating upon him of those not-to-be-avoided

impressions. Some of them at the source are most unprepossess-
ing. Certain others have lived so long in that "deep well" of his
unconsciousness that he can find no beginning for them. Others,
whose beginning he can identify, owe their existence to impressions which would be imperceptible to anyone besides
himself. Some of them seem to be barren until manipulated;
then, they all at once take fire. He demonstrates how he had let
them all, the big ones and the little ones, stew and simmer until they were ready for use.

Certain of these ideas he is able to identify as having taken
shape as a consequence of his habit of musing upon personalities. James' cousin, Mary Temple, stands a shadow behind Milly
Theale in *The Wings of the Dove*. A chance remark about John
Addington Symonds gave him the clue for *The Author of Beltraffio*. He used an unamiable side of Robert Browning for
Lord Mellifont in *The Private Life*. Samuel Taylor Coleridge
gave him the idea for Frank Saltram in *The Coxon Fund*. His
own emotion over England in 1869 was the basis of *A Passionate
Pilgrim*. The news that Jane Clairmont yet lived in Florence,
an old, old woman, gave him *The Aspern Papers*. The unfor-
gotten sight of an older man's reaching out to Paris flashed at
him all he needed to know to write *The Ambassadors*. A strange
boy upon a park bench became *Owen Wingrave*.

Less tangible than personalities were those situations, observed by him or casually reported to him by others, perhaps
as gossip, certain combinations and permutations of types, which
would strike fire in his mind. He would jot down samples for
future use. And since he was careless of anything but the for-
mula, the note, read today, might seem the dry dance of puppets.
But, in reserve, he held the flash, the fire of the imagination
which would light up this combination when called into play
by the right story. Such was his playing with the father-daughter
relationship which after years of fingering swelled into *The
Golden Bowl*. The dreadful *Turn of the Screw* grew out of an
arresting phrase about some children, the phrase telling no
story, only setting a mood.

The occasion might be anything, and in itself was unimpor-
tant. Its combination with other potent elements when worked
upon by the subjective imagination was everything. Suffice it to

say that, like Keats, every person, every object, every place pressed upon him its essential identity. And what persisted as a disturbance to his imagination must perforce be used.

And, through the experience of work over the years, James came to recognize a hard truth, which in the end became a shield: that the particular place no longer mattered, nor the time, nor the circumstance, because he could use anything. The worst as well as the best that might happen to him had no power to swerve him off his path, which was the right use (for fiction) of those happenings. He wrote to A. C. Benson in 1895 a kind of confession:

Just for today let me say that I think I find myself at the point where the difference between sadness and cheer, interest and detachment, lies behind in the road like a shuffled coil. It's all one, it's all life, it's all fate, it's all something.

The naïve practitioner of fiction believes that the life he has lived is the story he writes: so, the autobiographical novel; so, the eagerness to disguise the name, the detail, but then essentially to use the actual and the literal in one's stories. James' theory of fiction was entirely different, although his rapt attention for the world through which he moved might persuade one that he, too, contemplated moving it and all its trappings wholesale into his novels.

There are cases enough to be counted where the scene or the person in real life is visibly appropriated and placed in a short story or a novel. One case of the transfer of a likable landscape can be shown by comparing a letter and a story written shortly afterward. The scene, if not identical, is unmistakably built of the same items: the meadow, the stiles, and the rook-haunted church. The letter to his father dated March 19, 1870, notes a pure piece of Englishness in scenery,

where each square yard of ground lies verdantly brimming with the deepest British picturesque, and half begging, half deprecating a sketch. You should see how a certain stile broken footpath here winds through the meadows to a grey rook-haunted church.

In the story, *A Passionate Pilgrim*, Clement Searle, his England-loving hero, walks through that same scene:

Beyond the stile, across the level velvet of a meadow, a footpath lay, like a thread of darker woof. We followed it from field to field and from stile to stile. It was the way to church. At the church we finally arrived, lost in its rook-haunted churchyard, hidden from the workday world by the broad stillness of pastures.

It is probable that the writer's grandmother's house in Albany became Isabel Archer's house in Albany, the empty one in which she is discovered in solitude by her aunt. And it is even more likely that Mr. Henry James' house in Rye was the model for the house in which old Mr. Carteret dies and cuts off Nick Dormer from his fortune in *The Tragic Muse*. Milly Theale is an acknowledged homage to Mary Temple, James' cousin, who died young of tuberculosis. But saying this, one says almost nothing that is pertinent to James' idea of the connections between life and art, or of the relation between the literal (in life) and the true (in fiction).

However close the detail in the story is to the detail in the writer's life, is not important in itself. The truth recognized by James as inviolable is that once an item from life gets into a story, it is governed by a new set of rules. From that moment it exists as a part of the internal organization of that story. Its reference to something or someone, a personality, a place, or an incident, outside the scope of the story cannot be allowed as of any weight or the author can be accused rightly of cheating.

The case of the heroine of *The Wings of the Dove* is a good example because James identified her genesis with perfect frankness. There are striking similarities here between the actuality of life and the reality of art. Beyond a doubt, the essence of Milly Theale sprang from the deep impression made upon him by his cousin's living and dying as she did. The following words, written in memory of the real girl, Mary Temple, express perfectly the emotional impetus which pushed him into writing the novel:

She had beyond any equally young creature I have known a sense for verity of character and play of life in others, for their acting out of their force or their weakness, whatever either might be, at no matter what cost to herself; and it was this instinct that made her care so for life in general. . . . Life claimed her and used her and beset her —made her range in her groping, her naturally immature and unlighted way from end to end of the scale. . . . She was absolutely afraid of nothing she might come to by living with enough sincerity and enough wonder.

In addition to an attitude carried over to fiction from a particularly vivid experience in his actual living, there were numerous details: Mary Temple—Minnie, as he and William called her in their letters—had youth, grace, and imagination; so has Milly Theale; Minnie was an orphan; so is Milly, with parents, and indeed all the members of her family tragically dead; Minnie had the greatest capacity for life and died young; that fact is Milly's entire story.

Other elements, not so directly related to Mary Temple, can be seen (and how many must exist that cannot be traced) entering into the composition of the novel. There is something of Alice James, Henry's younger, gifted sister, in Milly Theale, as well as the concentrated essence of the entire "cousinage," of which Minnie Temple was the most exceptional member, who lived, all orphans, all bright, heedless, luckless, as contemporaries of the James children. And Milly is in part the representative of one of James' general ideas about beauty and youth and death. Without the leading idea, he might never have seized upon the instance and made such excellent use of it.

Underlining the resemblance between the author's life and the author's work goes a certain distance in explaining Henry James, but it does not explain the novel. Milly Theale in *The Wings of the Dove* lives (in the sense that a created character of fiction lives) not just as a reminder of a certain sick young woman the author knew in his youth, but as a part of a situation which is more complete than life and more stable and which has a different kind of momentum from the pace of actual living. She exists in an action which has a beginning, a middle, and an end. She exists in relation to various other created characters, Kate and Merton, Lord Mark, Mrs. Lowder, Sir Luke, and Mrs. Stringham, suggested no doubt by other unrelated experiences of the author, who have nothing to do with Henry James' dead cousin, but who, together with Milly, make up a satisfying and self-sustaining sphere of references, a kind of world.

If there are obvious similarities between the actual, dead girl and the living, fictional one, there are also striking differences. James gave his heroine a greater scope. He gave her Europe and society and success on a larger scale than Mary Temple attained in New York and Pelham. He gave her a spectacular rather than an adequate fortune. Certain attractive elements of Minnie's mind, her speculative cast, for instance, had to be shorn. For since art must always be truer than life, it must be more limited and more definite. Milly's mind is a simpler instrument than Minnie's, but within the rich, personal world which her creator gave her, its parts are more strikingly and poetically related to each other. She is necessarily more intense. Her person echoes and re-echoes the writer's sore persuasion that, "there plays inveterately within the beautiful, if it but go far enough, the fine strain of the tragic."

Milly was created, not just borrowed. She was evolved out of his moral consciousness, as he asserted, of another character, Miss Birdseye, whose reality was identified by some readers, including his brother, William, with the actuality of a certain Bostonian. If one sets the two portraits side by side, Mary Temple's in *Notes of a Son and Brother* and Milly Theale's in *The Wings of the Dove,* one sees how delicately James differentiated between the two kinds of art, the biographical and the fictional, and the respect which he had for both.

In the first, James set his cousin before one gently and persuasively by the humble addition of one selected fact to another. She was a part of his life, one acknowledged cause of his being the kind of Henry James he was, a memory, and an emotion treasured and finally spilled over in an unforgettable form in the final pages of *Notes of a Son and Brother.* Reading it, one sees James' gift for biography exercised at its highest pitch.

An appreciation of Minnie Temple is an extension of an appreciation of the author as a human being. The emotion with which one regards her grows and grows with every fact one adds to those already known about Henry, about his brother William, who also felt her influence, about their common friends, their old New York, about every faint ramification of their relationships, and their particular and conjoined lives. Unlike fiction, such an interest is not closely defined but is an indefinite extension of an interest in the writer's experience of life. It is legitimate for autobiography to be expression, but fiction must be primarily composition. A novel, by its nature, cannot be an expansion of the author's personal life: it is a form governed by laws alien to those ruling the actual and the literal.

That actuality from which the writer's imagination takes flight into the creative world of his stories is only a partially controllable element of his equipment. He cannot choose where to be born, nor when, nor the kinds of relatives and friends who will surround him in his formative years. He cannot choose his mental equipment nor the particular pattern impressions will take upon entering his mind. By the time he reaches maturity and assumes the posture of a writer, much of his attitude toward life has been determined already. One should take account of these mostly unconscious habits of the mind—whether one is romantic or realistic; whether one has a sense of humor; whether one is tragic or comic or neither—for together these almost unseizable elements of an artist's being make his tone. They form the impalpable envelope in which his stories are packaged.

Alfred North Whitehead once divided the process of learning into a natural rhythm of three recurring stages: (1) romance, (2) precision, and (3) generalization. Here is the way he traces that rhythmical development:

> The stage of romance is the stage of first apprehension. The subject matter has the vividness of novelty; it holds within itself unexplored connexions with possibilities half-disclosed by glimpses and half concealed by the wealth of material.
>
> The stage of precision also represents an addition to knowledge. In this stage, wealth of relationship is subordinated to exactness of formulation. . . . It is evident that a stage of precision is barren without a previous stage of romance.
>
> The final stage of generalisation is Hegel's synthesis. It is a return to romanticism with added advantage of classified ideas and relevant technique. It is the fruition which has been the goal of the precise training. It is the final success.

I have included these words of Whitehead's not to show that James was scientific, for he was not, but to show that the artist's bungling, wasteful, unscientific, extremely personal development can, after the fact, display a relevant relationship to a general truth stated by a scientist and developed by scientific method. Art and science, if they go far enough, reinforce each other. The grandiose world of the modern scientist and the mysterious world of the modern novelist establish a relationship, one to the other, in this meeting.

For James' education in his art developed by Whitehead's progression. The pieces written before the discovery of Europe, stories such as *Poor Richard, A Landscape Painter, A Day of Days,* dating from 1866 to 1869, hardly count. They are respectably well written and show a talent for psychological analysis, but they are too modest. They lack passion. "Europe" gave him that, and the exhilaration to go beyond careful cleverness. An outburst of writing followed the stimulus of the trip of 1869–1870: *Roderick Hudson, The American,* among the novels, and *A Passionate Pilgrim, The Madonna of the Future,* and *Daisy Miller,* among numerous stories, owe their existence to a youthful, romantic emotion.

James at that period was full of freshness of feeling and unashamed of his enthusiasm. The emotion expressed in *A Passionate Pilgrim* by its hero is the author's as well:

There is a rare emotion, familiar to every intelligent traveller, in which the mind, with a great passionate throb, achieves a magical synthesis of its impressions. You feel England; you feel Italy.

We greeted these things [the sights and sounds of England] as children greet the loved pictures in a story-book, lost and mourned and found again.

As the years passed, he consolidated his materials and his emotions. He saw more kinds of people walking upon the European (and American) scene than he had discovered at first glance. He came to speak to them as compatriots of his imagination. He came to know what caused them to behave as they did. He stood among them, more earthbound than he had been, seeing them at close range, handling them with familiarity and fluency. Characteristic novels of this time are *The Bostonians, The Princess Casamassima, The Tragic Muse, The Spoils of Poynton, What Maisie Knew,* and *The Awkward Age.* They are all concerned with a great many things, social activities and scenes, reform, revolution, the theater, property, divorce and marriage. They are more bound down to the ordinary social scale than he had seemed to be before or was to be later. These novels are rich in detail and harmonious in color; that world, which he had claimed at a glance years before, had been peopled. In these stories he is exact, even painful in his analysis of the motives of human nature. His understanding of his characters is comprehensive and impartial. He is, for him, realistic.

If one compares this group of novels with those which came before, and those after, a striking and obvious difference is visible. It is romance at both ends of the career, with realism in the middle. But the difference between the romance of the late period and of the early one is a great one. The late novels, *The Sacred Fount, The Wings of the Dove, The Ambassadors, The Golden Bowl, The Sense of the Past,* and *The Ivory Tower* have the benefit of the rich experience of life which went into the middle period of living and writing. Their romance is impregnated with realism. Their author, by the time he had come to write them, had got knowledge, got wisdom, and earned freedom.

After the fact of writing them and almost forgetting them, James could sit down and analyze the early works and hit off a general truth in definition of their qualities. The particular criticism which the preface writer of 1908 had for *The American* was just the fact that it was too romantic. Its experience of life appeared to be unrelated. It was experience "liberated, so to speak; experience disengaged, disembroiled, disencumbered, exempt from the conditions that we usually know to attach to it, and, if we wish so to put the matter, drag upon it."

The difficult author of 1908 required a different kind of intensity—"the greatest intensity"—"when the sacrifice of community, of the 'related' sides of situations, has not been too rash." To expect that intensity of *The American* was to ask too much, but he did find that it conformed to a different standard, the romancer's. He invented a figure to make plain the experience with which the romancer had to do—a balloon floating high above the earth whose rope, the rope by which "we know where we are," has been cut for the fun of it. In this novel he found such a case:

What I have recognized then in *The American,* much to my surprise and after long years, is that the experience here represented is the disconnected and uncontrolled experience—uncontrolled by our general sense of "the way things happen"—which romance more or less successfully palms off on us.

The author's criticism stands. The book is not "realistic." The motivation of the gigantic swindle worked upon the hero by the Bellegardes is not reasonable. The family, the formidable collection of Bellegardes, seems, in the end, gratuitously proud and wicked. This is true in spite of the fact that James has presented them in a series of striking poses. Also, Claire, the heroine and daughter of the Bellegardes, seems little more than a graceful, ineffectual shadow. In trying not to make her contemptible (in accepting and rejecting Newman), James succeeded only in making her mysterious.

Newman, himself, is made of good sound timber, but he is as stiff as the material of which he is made. He is never as living as Valentin, for instance, who is the best creation of the book. James furnished his millionaire American with plausible references to his past, references to killings in Wall Street, to his having once manufactured washtubs, to his having served as a general in the Civil War; yet that past never quite lives. James had yet to do the American businessman well, and was to do so in *The Golden Bowl* and *The Ivory Tower*. He was not equipped to do it in 1877, when he wrote *The American*.

Yet *The American* deserves justice. Its action goes with a rush and a steady gathering of suspense. Its alternatives are melodramatically simple. The reader hurries through it, his eyes shut to serious faults, for the pleasure of finding out what happens next; desiring to know whether Newman revenges himself upon the family, or rescues Claire from the convent. It is as clean-cut as that.

James, thirty-one years later, gave the younger writer due credit:

I had been plotting arch-romance without knowing it . . . the thing is consistently, consummately—and I would fain make bold to say charmingly—romantic; and all without intention, presumption, hesitation, contrition . . . and I lose myself, at this late hour, I am bound to say in a certain sad envy of the free play of so much unchallenged instinct.

Roderick Hudson, written two years before *The American*, is a more successful, if even more naked victory of the natural romanticism of the young author. If it has a flaw, for the kind of piece it is, it is the fact that Roderick, its hero, goes a little too straight to his right romantic doom. He had said, "If I break down . . . I shall stay down." And so he does. He skyrockets into his brief career and falls back to earth in a graceful arc, with only those circumstances stressed which make the story pathetic and affecting. It is not that "the way things happen" is entirely missing—witness the mother and Mary Garland and Rowland Mallett, who are skillfully and realistically done—but that this element is muted, played low before the one emphatic note of Roderick's personality and Roderick's fate.

By the time James wrote *The Awkward Age* (the publication date of this novel is 1899), he was obviously very conscious of "the way things happen." The difference between its hero, Vanderbank, and the earlier Roderick or Newman, is that in this more involved case the reader is never allowed to lose sight of "old Van's" circumstances. He is as exceptional a hero, as gifted, as shining a young man as they, yet he is always seen in relation to people: Mrs. Brook, Mitchy, Nanda, Mr. Longdon; or to certain lucky or unlucky circumstances: his lack of money, his good looks, his knowledge of the world, his ignorance of Nanda's heart. They close him in until the undeniable charm he has, the special quality to which the others pay tribute as "the sacred terror," begins to echo with a note of irony.

If Roderick, in 1875, is James' romantic hero, and Vanderbank, in 1899, is his realistic hero, what is Ralph Pendrel in *The Sense of the Past*—unfinished at the time of the writer's death in 1916? It seems at first glance that Ralph must be romantic, for what does "the way things happen" have to do with a young man who makes an expedition into the past? But it is only the events which are fantastic. The character is grounded in the sense of reality. The reasons for Ralph's doing this or that carry the consideration of seventy years of living. He wrote the same story once before in *A Passionate Pilgrim* in 1870. To compare the two is to compare his entire development. One is all innocent expression, the other, all considered composition. Yet the later story is more fantastic than the first. And they are both ghost stories of a kind.

The theme of the late novel is identical with that of the early story, a falling in love with the past upon the part of an ardent,

young, New World gentleman. The instigation of this obsession
is in both cases an old house. There is a picture in each story with
which the hero identifies himself; he says that that, upon the
wall, is what he might have been. Searle, in *A Passionate Pilgrim,*
fancies the life he might have lived, when idleness and mental
vagrancy were not criminal. But Searle only wishes and dies in a
brief delirium in which he dreams himself into his ancestor's
place. Ralph, in *The Sense of the Past,* resolves his fantasy more
sensibly. He walks by daylight (late afternoon, to be sure) into
the house and into the action of the past. The older James was
not afraid to be unrealistic in circumstance if, in doing so, he
could get nearer to a solution of Ralph's motives. *A Passionate
Pilgrim* objectifies a sick desire and nothing more. *The Sense of
the Past* demonstrates strict consequences. The novel, if it had
been finished, would have analyzed, from the inside, that illness
of the mind which Ralph showed in romanticizing the past: he
was to come to feel a nausea for the alien time in which he was
trapped. The reader was to accompany Ralph through the past
and out again. The obsession was to be seen entire: so much can
be seen in the writer's notes for the complete book.

The difference is the fact that the characters, not Ralph Pendrel alone, but those others he finds in the past, Mrs. Midmore
of Drydown, Molly and Nan and Sir Cantopher Bland, are real.
The author's understanding of them is not fantastic but accurate,
and neither flattering nor unflattering. He can afford once again
to be romantic in his trappings. He has at his fingertips the
weight of years of experience. In this novel, and in all the other
late ones, he carries his authority gracefully. He can dare what he
never attempted in the middle years, a richness of poetry and
fantasy which is related with affecting solidity to the all important "way things happen." He can be as romantic as he likes,
since the core of action is true. His truth, as developed in the
great late novels, has the flexibility of use and can dispense with
the props of laborious documentation.

Early romantic and late romantic—but the point is labored if
one attempts to make the divisions clean-cut. There is a kind of
realism in the late works even when they are devoid of realistic
method. And, upon the other hand, his realism of the time of the
middle period is too partial and tender to be complete. His

youthful romanticism had perspective, of a sort, and so was not entirely romantic. For example, the author presents Roderick Hudson as a romantic figure and does so with wholehearted enthusiasm. Yet he is not taken in by Roderick's own estimation of life. In this early novel, where one would least expect it, is a classic definition of romanticism in this cool description of Roderick himself:

> The great and characteristic point with him was the perfect separateness of his sensibility. He never saw himself as part of the whole; only as the clear-cut, sharp-edged, isolated individual, rejoicing or raging, as the case might be, but needing in any case absolutely to affirm himself.

In the long variety and succession of his books, James moved about restlessly, in and out of various formulas, never letting himself be pinned under one label. He has a fluidity that is an agreeable contrast to the shrill partisans of strict allegiances. He never tried to be any particular kind of writer (except a responsible one) and never belonged to a school. He found the great difficulty to be faced was the direct apprehension of life. He tried a great many ways of reflecting that quality upon the pages of his books.

He had the advantage of a sense of humor, an attitude which helped to shape his fiction. What is his humor? It is the perception of the incongruous, the self-deceiving, the overreaching, or the false; and, in operation, a delicate tool of the spirit that waives method, makes lightning-quick distinctions, cuts through apparent obstacles, and finds the quickest way to the center of reality. It can be looked at in two ways: with distrust, since humor is a part of the irreverent irresponsibility of the artist; and with respect, for it is a short cut to the truth; a smile or a laugh acts as a quick way to "the way things happen." It is all one: the irreverence is as necessary as the prompt respect for the truth.

The irreverent turn of mind came to James by legitimate inheritance. His father had it. Henry James, Sr.'s private description of Longfellow was "good inoffensive comforting Longfellow." His son's comment upon Walter Pater, in the same vein, was "well, faint, pale, embarrassed, exquisite Pater!"

One function of humor is to disturb. Since words can make respectability uneasy and the established shaky, it seems, with a handful of casually gathered samples before one, that humor is altogether a matter of words, the rhythm, the suggestiveness, and the power of words. One can destroy a concept by an adjective, "direst propriety"; or by an adverb, "the fatuously fortunate." One can rise above the serious by the gesture of a pun; he discusses the means of making "functional love" "interesting, and productive (I don't mean *re*productive!")". And one can slide down a sharp descent in the emphasis of anticlimax: "He has a genius for upholstery"; or: "His very beauty was the beauty of the grocer." There is the elaborate wit of deliberate circumlocution: "The widow of a nephew of his father," and the wit of sudden deflation:

Her misfortunes were three in number: first, she had lost her husband; second, she had lost her money, or the greater part of it; and third, she lived at Northampton, Massachusetts.

There is the organ tone of the mock-serious:

and of course one would never have seen him at his finest if one hadn't seen him in his remorses. They set in mainly at this season and were magnificent, elemental, orchestral.

There is the broken rhythm which is almost the cause of the wit (the sound of the phrase being as important as its sense):

She was not familiar with her children's governess; she was not even familiar with her children themselves.

There is the indecorous contrast of

nurses . . . who, with their black uniforms and fresh faces of business, suggested the barmaid emulating the nun.

And there is the freeness of unregulated speech (and mind):

You can let your conscience alone if you're nice to the second housemaid.

Without the smile, some of the novels and short stories would hardly have reason to exist. Any keen perception of social manners is of necessity humorous. It is a part of the nature of human customs, especially the old and established ones, to seem not altogether serious to anyone with a degree of perspective. Part of James' fun in the international stories was in seeing Europe with American eyes and America with European eyes. In that way and with a good will, he could offend Philistines on both sides of the Atlantic. That was his accomplishment with the treacherous wit of stories like *An International Episode, Lady Barberina,* and *The Siege of London.* Since his fun is not cruel, being allied to a tender concern for the person buried under the weight of custom, the result is not a serious disgust with custom, but an amused toleration and enjoyment of it.

The Europeans is as good an example as possible of the lighter foolery in which James could indulge. In it he derides both European elaborateness and New England unfurnished seriousness. It is a small thing compared to the two preceding, ambitious, romantic novels, *Roderick Hudson* and *The American,* yet *The Europeans* has its virtues. It is neat, witty, apposite, and a direct turnabout in the use of material. In this story two Europeans, an older sister and a brother, come to the New World, to rural Massachusetts, to conquer their local relatives. But the idle, gay, flippant young sketcher, the brother, Felix Young, falls in love with his cousin, Gertrude Wentworth, finding her more charming, stronger, and more full of temperament than any European woman he had ever met; while the Countess, his sister, the morganatic wife of an improbable Prince Adolf of Silberstadt-Schreckenstein, disturbs everyone considerably, helping to bring about three weddings by her unsettling presence, but personally is not quite the success she had planned. Gertrude's younger brother, Clifford, ends by being embarrassed by her and rushing into the arms of a local sweetheart. Robert Acton, who is considered the man of the world of the community, is charmed and curious, but finding that the Countess lies, thinks better of his curiosity.

One laughs at the Countess for being involved with the rustic Wentworths, and the Wentworths for being involved with her. Most of the laughter is at the expense of the Countess Eugenia, for overreaching and overestimating herself. The theme of the book is the importance of frivolity. Gertrude Wentworth, like Verena Tarrant, in *The Bostonians,* awakens to the delight of being frivolous, of loving, and of discarding the sense of duty as the motive of living. Felix is a laughing mood and not much besides. He and the sister, Eugenia, are good samples of the type of adventurer who appears and reappears in one novel after another.

James could never write about New England with a straight face. The story is full of fun at the expense of sectional rigidity. But he also does the sober, bare, *nice,* country atmosphere full justice. The two houses described, the Wentworth's and the Acton's, are staidly prosperous and coolly modest. They contrast favorably to the Countess' chalet, as she calls her cottage across the road from the Wentworths', in which she drapes her dirty furbelows.

The style is almost giddy, very delicate and light. Mr. Wentworth, the father, finds that "The strange word 'morganatic,' was constantly in his ears; it reminded him of a certain Mrs. Morgan whom he had once known and who had been a bold, unpleasant woman." The story is a bubble of wit, hollow but very pretty; however, it is a *little* style for James. This novel, *The Europeans,* is much closer in tone to the comedy of manners than anything else he wrote. The characters are manipulated with ease while those of the later novels have the force, weight, and sometimes the inertia of real people. *The Europeans* does not have much weight. It is more a web of words, thrown into the air and shaken into a pattern. And hardly a sentence, a phrase, or a word but shines with laughter.

James accepts the fact that people are inevitably stuck in society and that there is no way of getting them out. A great deal of his humor is social, an exhibit of alien social verities solemnly clashing; or his favorite way, the exhibit of the new man in the old society. Coexistent with the easier laughter is the more fundamental and unhappy laughter of the falsity of the human creature, who is, after all, only superficially clothed by the costume of time, place, and circumstance. The two degrees of humor are not segregated; they operate simultaneously. The trivial and the terrific come into the same room (often, a drawing room in James) and sit down together, as they do in their improper way in life.

James has many ways of demonstrating the sad folly of his people: by the arrangement of a scene; by the sequence of exits and entrances; by strange juxtapositions; or by the rhythm of his words; and, one of his best means, by the use of the fool. By "fool," one means the intelligent, witty, sad, disengaged character, half in, half out of the story, who looks on at the action and comments upon it. He is disqualified, for some reason, physical or spiritual, for the main action himself, and so, half-creature that he is, makes more emphatic the whole men and women who turn to him for distraction or enlightenment.

In the early novel *Roderick Hudson,* Christina Light moves across its pages not just as a beautiful girl, but as an admirable, disconnected jester. Passive to her own bad fortune, she lets her idle tongue hurt whom it will with unpalatable truths. But she becomes interested in Roderick and in mischief-making and so disqualifies herself as fool. Valentin, in *The American,* is another part-time fool. In a kind of private despair at a wasted life, and yet resigned to the waste, he hits with words at the cause, his family. But he removes himself out of foolery and out of life by a quixotic duel which ties up all the loose threads of his existence.

Ralph Touchett, Isabel Archer's cousin in *The Portrait of a Lady,* is one of the best of fools, as well as men. Dying of tuberculosis, exempt from living, although unable to get quickly out of it; in love, yet concealing it; he speaks truth in his ugly jokes. "Clever and ill—a combination by no means felicitous—" Ralph is criticized by his father and answers for himself and the other fools:

"You young men have too many jokes. When there are no jokes you've nothing left."

"Fortunately there are always more jokes," the ugly young man remarked.

"I don't believe it—I believe things are getting more serious. You young men will find that out."

"The increased seriousness of things, then—that's the great opportunity of jokes."

To continue the roll call, there is Gabriel Nash, the perfect and complete aesthete of *The Tragic Muse,* who is of no use in himself but an excellent touchstone for others. He has severed relations with life, but as Nick Dormer's jester, assists Nick in a crucial moment to make a transfer from the public to the private life. When Nick begins to act for himself and to insist that Gabriel be a real person, then the imperturbable Nash fades out, disappears over the horizon. And Nick, who had entreated his friend, "Don't melt away," wonders "if he hadn't at last, balancing always on the stretched tight-rope of his wit, fallen over on the wrong side."

The Gnome and the Giant—Mitchy, in *The Awkward Age,* thus names his relationship to Lord Petherton. He is, of course, in his own mind, the Gnome. Disappointed in his private desires, he prostitutes his good nature in assisting the rapacious man in a display of arrogant living. Himself ugly, rich (there is his usefulness), and clever, Mitchy finds a kind of amusement in being used. But his suffering is apparent for all the wit he uses to distract his audience, Mrs. Brooks' drawing-room coterie. Mitchenden, the man behind the ugly body, is the most painful of the fools.

Any pause before the comic leads one straight to the other extreme of the tragic. They often live side by side in James, as in Valentin's death in *The American.* Newman asks him, " 'And how are you getting on?' " And he answers, " 'Oh, I'm getting off!' " He continues to joke about Newman's fantastic proposition, made once, to carry him off to America and place him in a bank:

"I am rather sorry about that place in the bank. Who knows but that I might have become another Rothschild? But I wasn't meant for a banker; bankers are not so easy to kill. Don't you think I have been very easy to kill? It's not like a serious man. It's really very mortifying. It's like telling your hostess you must go, when you count upon her begging you to stay, and then finding she does no such thing. 'Really—so soon? You've only just come!' Life doesn't make me any such polite little speech."

Always in James there is the insolent bravery of the unserious erupting in the face of the serious. Sometimes the joke is almost completely sad, as when Merton Densher, in *The Wings of the Dove,* is the only one, the one beloved by Milly, who cannot see her as a "Princess," but only as a funny little American girl with red hair. Revenge (not Milly's, for she is dead) is complete. He sees her, once she is underground, for the personage that she was. He hears his doom pronounced by Kate, and acquiesces:

"I used to call her, in my stupidity—for want of anything better—a dove. Well she stretched out her wings, and it was to *that* they reached. They cover us."

"They cover us," Densher said.

It is hopeless to try to unravel the threads of the comic and tragic. In James they are the different facets of the same truth. Each light reflects its opposite shadow for those who can see.

Ralph Touchett provides the wit of *The Portrait of a Lady,* yet his living and dying as he does is a kind of reference to reality for Isabel. In the end she comes to him as to a verity. Valentin's smiles crack the hard plate of falsity in which his family lives; and he is most deadly serious when, dying, he apologizes to Newman for them and for what they have done to his friend. Even Gabriel Nash has his one instant of being immovably solid and true when he tells Nick what art is and what duty, for the artist, is:

"We must recognize our particular form, the instrument that each of us—each of us who carries anything—carries in his being. Mastering this instrument, learning to play it in perfection—that's what I call duty, what I call conduct, what I call success!"

"I see, I see [says Nick]. And what might your instrument be?"

Nash hesitated not a moment; his answer was radiantly there. "To speak to people just as I'm speaking to you—I say the things other people don't, the things they can't, the things they won't."

In *The Awkward Age,* it is obvious that Mitchenden is good; even Mrs. Brook sees that fact, as a joke, and thus characterizes him to his face:

"You're the most delicate thing I know, and it crops up with effect the oddest in the intervals of your corruption. Your talk's half the time impossible; you respect neither age nor sex nor condition; one doesn't know what you'll say or do next; and one has to return you books—*c'est tout dire*—under cover of darkness. Yet there's in the midst of all this and in the general abyss of you a little deep down delicious niceness, a sweet sensibility."

Nothing is plain black or white. Pursue laughter, you get tears. Hunt the beautiful, you get the tragic. He gives one none of these qualities in stark simplicity. They all partake of each other in his world, which is a mixed universe.

So he comes to see as a principle that "there plays inveterately within the beautiful, if it but go far enough, the fine strain of the tragic." This fact is what he brings his reader to see in Isabel Archer, Hyacinth Robinson, Milly Theale, or Lambert Strether; in any characteristic person or action which he presents in a sustained emphasis. He *must* end on this note; given his nature, and the frankness of facing that person who was himself, there was no other place he could come out.

This mixture (ambiguity is the word he liked) operates with potency not only inside the world of fiction, but within his personal world of work. He was conscious always of the contradiction of "the precious effect dreadful to lose and yet impossible to render which interfused the aesthetic dream in presence of its subject with the mortal drop of despair." Art was not only beneficent and mighty, it was also "the uncanny principle." And the treacherous mind found "Europe" the source of a many-colored truth, also a kind of poison; the fascination felt from childhood for the old was "the deeply infected state."

Awakening means losing one's innocence. The artist cannot be innocent. He is forever outside Eden. Evil and good, the mixture, pair themselves before his probing eyes as he sees them in "the way things happen."

PART *Six*

Means

THE UNCONSCIOUS ELEMENTS OF THE ARTIST'S NATURE DIS-
cussed in Part Five are really no business of the artist-
worker. He knows that they exist and that they help shape his
books; he pays them his due and humble respects, gives himself
a shake, and sets himself to concentrate upon those elements of
his work which are controllable.

The aim of this chapter is to consider the tools of the craft,
what in working with them Henry James attempted, and what
he accomplished. But first, see what the struggle—so little of
which he let anyone see—did to him. He did not believe in keeping the door ajar, the door to the writer's study where he had his
despairs and ecstasies. He opened it only a crack many years later
when he deliberately exhibited certain cases in cold blood in the
Prefaces of the 1908 edition.

The nature of the effort, and it was a real struggle, with elements which were always more powerful than he, imposed a
particular kind of character upon him. It was a graceless character in relation to the work. However social an animal James
was in every other respect, as concerned the work, he was solitary,
individual, and dissociated.

Invited once, by John Bailey, to be chairman of the English
Association, he refused in a way to make clear his position upon
joining and associating:

For me, frankly, my dear John, there is simply no question of these
things: I am a mere stony, ugly monster of *Dis*sociation and Detach-

ment. I have never in all my life gone in for these things, but have dodged and shirked and successfully evaded them . . . the rough sense of it is that I believe only in absolutely independent, individual and lonely virtue, and in the serenely unsociable (or if need be at a pinch sulky and sullen) practice of the same; the observation of a lifetime having convinced me that no fruit ripens but under that temporarily graceless rigour, and that the associational process for bringing it on is but a bright and hollow artifice, all vain and de-lusive. (I speak here of the Arts—or of my own attempt at one or two of them; the other matters must speak for themselves.)

The attitude toward the world of joiners was uncompromis-ing. Looking inward, instead of outward, the artist's attitude toward his own work was also unconciliating; "Art should be as hard as nails—as hard as the heart of the artist." These are the two sides of his hardness.

As far as the work was concerned, the artist must see all round his creatures. He must enjoy the mean, the ugly, and the bad as well as he does the graceful and the good. James had natively this necessary artist's gusto for the "done." He called his villainous strokes lovely and his disasters delightful. A symptom of the hard-heartedness necessary to the craft was his matter-of-fact discus-sion of the efficacy of illness in moving not his, but the reader's heart:

as if to be menaced with death or danger hadn't been from time im-memorial, for heroine or hero, the very shortest of all cuts to the interesting state. . . . The process of life gives way fighting, and often may so shine out on the lost ground as in no other connexion. One had had moreover, as a various chronicler, one's secondary physi-cal weaklings and failures, one's accessory invalids—

And so, he says, in conclusion, Milly Theale's sickness in *The Wings of the Dove* works for the general engrossment of the reader in her case. (James was making a case here, unconsciously, for pathos rather than for tragedy. His entire work can be seen as the highest achievement possible of pathos, an achievement which just lacks the greatest power of genuine tragedy.) On his own ground, he was as efficient as he thought himself to be. He was an economist in effect. He did what he intended to do.

These are the qualities which it is good for the artist to have:

the single mind, the hard heart, and the fanatical aim. If they are compounded in the right proportions with talent and a frank openness to impressions, they reward him with a compensation, the artist's peace of mind: "The artist's serenity . . . an intellectual and spiritual capital that must never brook defeat—which it so easily might incur by a single act of abdication."

The worker's coming to terms with himself upon the subject of his own work means strength. Whatever the world does or says, he has this peace of uncompromised and uncompromising work. The touch of fanaticism, mentioned already as necessary, is like the cold water into which the steel is plunged to temper and strengthen it. And add to fanaticism the pride of the artist in the work done. That work, a daily sitting down at a desk to spin a something out of nothing, to make believe, is trash to the world, but to him it is an act of belief, belief in the importance of the useless. "Be as melancholy as you like," James said once, "—but try to be as perfect an artifex, for there is always glee in that and it is the best resistance to fate."

James was lucky in his lifetime that he never had to "abdicate" from that serenity; unlucky were those, like Rimbaud in France and, later, Hart Crane in America, who found in their time, their place, their circumstances, and perhaps in themselves an element which made abdication necessary and achievement impossible. What can be said for these Ishmaels of art is that they made more of the act of abdication than many others made of achievement. It is worth repeating that James was almost the last of the artists of the century who could be happy and whole in his work.

If the artist consisted only in prideful solitude, satisfied hardness, and imperturbable serenity, then the portrait would be that of a monster. The saving grace is the faculty of criticism. It was just the fact that James pulled criticism into the circle of creation (and never felt its presence there as hateful) which distinguished him and saved him from fatuousness.

He described in an early page of the *Notes of a Son and Brother* the mixture of emotions he had felt as a young man awakening to glory and to art, as so many of his young heroes were to do, and unselfconsciously admitted the critical in the same breath as he did the other necessities: "To feel a unity . . . to face the aesthetic, the creative, even quite wondrously, the critical life," was his manner of becoming more alive.

Criticism was not a profanation of creativity. Creation was not shy, but healthy and assertive. It could afford to make the acquaintance of the rude, destructive spirit of the opposite, or the supposedly opposite, faculty. He said genially, "I am *damned* critical—but it's the only thing to be and all else is damned humbug."

Superficial difficulties have obscured the fact of Henry James' undoubted, real success as a writer. Attentive reading, however, leads one inexorably to the fact of that success. Futher study convinces that the success is due to two obvious virtues working together: narrative power and understanding of character.

The success is not mysterious, but simple. James grasped, or had inborn, the ability to tell a story. The short story or novel as it developed in his hands has a backbone or a structure, a subject which is simple enough to have shock value; a story of his is emphatically not just an impression or portrait or slice of life. It is a definite happening or action.

He possessed also the other virtue, which in many writers of fiction excludes, or is excluded by, the first, the insight into mentality. The understanding of the abysmal complexity of the human mind and the demonstration of its workings sets up a healthy tension vying with the purer motive of getting on with the story. The operation of the two virtues in proper proportion, one to the other, makes for rich, complex, dynamic fiction. Parenthetically, James' insight into the human interior is expressed by him in terms friendly to storytelling, that is, in images and objective renderings of actions and thoughts—for thought is a form of action in his stories. His fiction encompassed his generation's science of the mind. (We have his word for it that he read William James.) But his expression of that knowledge is science disguised.

Any novel of James' would illustrate two planes of interest. In *What Maisie Knew* the reader never becomes indifferent to the actual, physical disposal of Maisie. As the poor child, the formidable child, is tossed with an increasing momentum from one to another of the five adults who share and shirk her care, there is an intensification of the question: What will become of Maisie?

Allied to this concern for the bodily disposition of Maisie Farrange is the more puzzling question of her moral fate: What and how much has she come to understand of the undignified scramble in the midst of which she has been passed about from hand to hand?

The two poles of interest are what happens and what that happening means to the person involved. The story has movement forward, and it has, as it moves, a subtle contraction or gathering to itself of richness. The difficulty with James is that he has got the cart before the horse. The richness is obvious. That rich complexity has too often baffled the way to the discovery of the austere, single-minded drive forward of the narrative.

To go on with cases: In *The Portrait of a Lady* the onlooker wants (first) to know the simple answer to an easy question, which suitor Isabel will marry; and (second) he wants to know the difficult answer to a subtle question, what, when married, Isabel will make of her vaunted freedom. In *The Spoils of Poynton* the onlooker wonders who, mother or son, will gain the final grasp upon the splendid sticks and shreds of furniture; and also, what the cruel tussle between blood relatives for the possession of property can signify. Whatever skill James developed had a direct reference to these two elements of interest: the force of the story's action, the significance of the character's reaction.

Achievement in narration and achievement in psychological analysis cannot be separated in James. They are attributes of each other and the end of all the effort of whatever cunning means he possessed. But it is a help, in attempting to understand the writer's means, from the humblest to the most pretentious, to take those means, one by one, on an ascending ladder of complexity, as tools used for the accomplishment of the two ends of his labor: the realization of action, the realization of character.

It is a native, childlike quality in man to be pleased by a story. A pattern of words, which is also a pattern of events and ideas, satisfies a deep need. The sense of story, a certain rhythm of interest building to a climax and resolving into finality after passing through that agony, is an elemental pleasure. In achieving this sense of story, James made use of both the entirely respectable elements of narrative and the shady gifts of melodrama.

To note an indispensable quality first, he had the necessary gift of timing. Through the use of foresight, suspense, surprise, hindsight, and related elements, James was able to achieve this principal requirement of good fiction. The reader is picked up with a rush of interest; then retarded; baffled, perhaps; rewarded for his curiosity; surprised, even shocked; and, in the end, satisfied. The means by which the writer achieved this retarding or accelerating of interest appear, upon the surface of the story, as unforeseen, and once past, inevitable. When the sense of inevitability is lacking, as in the conclusion of *The American,* then the novel seems, in retrospect, to be flat and something of a cheat. In the successful story, and however difficult many of them are, upon their own terms they are successful; the alternation of expectation and satisfaction is as natural as breathing. The gift not only makes possible the telling of a convincing story, it makes the characters who enact the story seem poignant. Their dilemmas are probable enough for belief and uncertain enough for concern.

In the first place, James was fair to the reader's initial curiosity. He was even generous to it. Roderick Hudson's future can be read into the first description of him to appear in the novel bearing his name:

> The fault of the young man's whole structure was an excessive want of breadth. The forehead, though high and brave, was narrow, the jaw and the shoulders were narrow, and the result was an air of insufficient physical substance [but] . . . certainly there was life enough in his eye to furnish an immortality.

At the beginning of *The Portrait of a Lady,* Ralph Touchett, who will give Isabel Archer a fortune, gives her his dog. The incident is a natural, unceremonious manifestation of the man's character. And in the early pages of *The Golden Bowl,* Maggie Verver, who has had no troubles, who has a loving father, an attentive fiancé, and a cushioned position, curiously proclaims that it is her nature "to tremble for my life. That's the way I live!" The novel grimly makes clear to Maggie from that page to the end a justification for her unreasoned conviction.

The writer's method is first a generous hint for engrossment, then the operation of suspense to balance that openness and exert a cross-tension. In Roderick's case, where the foreboding note is sounded in the early pages, the anticipation of disaster soon gives way to delight in his brilliant, reckless accomplishments. When uneasiness creeps in, it is in dread of a sudden end of his glory. *The Portrait of a Lady* and *The Golden Bowl* are both novels of deception. The suspense in them concerns itself with the end of security for the two heroines.

Surprise is an element of suspense, or rather it is the climax of suspense. Shock ends one phase of action and begins another. Roderick, learning of Christina's treachery, abandons ambition and gives himself up to regret and inanition. Contrariwise, Maggie, upon proof of the deception practiced upon her, begins to crawl, step by step, out of the comfortable hole dug for her by husband and friend.

A variation in the speed of the story is the writer's use of a pause in the time scheme. He makes use of what might be called frozen moments for emphasis, for intensity, for value. For example, the fateful governess in *The Turn of the Screw*, approaching the house in which she is to be sorely tried, undergoes one of these lapses in time:

> The place, moreover, in the strangest way in the world, had, on the instant, and by the very fact of its appearance, become a solitude. To me at least, making my statement here with a deliberation with which I have never made it, the whole feeling of the moment returns. It was as if, while I took it in—what I did take in—all the rest of the scene had been stricken with death. I can hear again, as I write, the intense hush in which the sounds of the evening dropped. The rooks stopped cawing in the golden sky and the friendly hour lost, for the minute, all its voice.

In the other novels, where there is no suggestion of the supernatural as there is in *The Turn of the Screw*, he employs the pause in time to accommodate an expansion of the emotions of a character who is at that instant in a crisis of some kind. A good early example of such an instant is one involving Nora Lambert in *Watch and Ward*:

> Nora felt as if she had taken a jump, and was learning in mid-air that the distance was tenfold what she had imagined. It is strange how the hinging-point of great emotions may rest on an instant of time. These instants, however, seem ages, viewed from within; and in

such a reverberating moment Nora felt something that she had believed to be a passion melting from beneath her feet, crumbling and crashing into the gulf on whose edge she stood.

What James achieved in these "reverberating" moments was the texture of thought itself. He made the reader experience simultaneously with the character the sights, sounds, and smells associated with the explosion into being of an idea and an emotion. Roderick's prostration, Milly's sentence of death, Maggie's shattered marriage, Strether's last chance to come alive, all reverberate for the reader because he lives these moments at length and in detail.

Certain key words identify the ineffability and the timelessness of the experience:

Roderick—lying there like a Buddhist in an intellectual swoon, a deep dreamer whose perception should be slowly ebbing back to temporal matters.

Milly—she went forward into space. . . . She was borne up for the hour.

Maggie—there in silence she felt within her the sudden split between conviction and action.

Strether—his perception of the man's identity . . . had been quite one of the sensations that count in life; he had certainly never known one that had acted, as he might have said, with a more crowded rush. . . . He was in presence of a fact that occupied his whole mind.

The device is artificial, of course, and it skirts near to the danger of seeming to be so. But used sparingly and effectively, as it is in general, it concentrates the flow of action into knots of effective meaning. It is only at the very end of his career that the method becomes a nuisance, as in *The Sense of the Past,* where the entire narrative is a succession of frozen moments. This fact gives that novel an exasperating intensity and a glacial slowness. The progress of an instant of time takes on the fullness and completeness of an hour of living; an hour swells to a day, and one day stretches endlessly across the pages of the book.

But when the device is used in moderation, it serves a definite purpose, both in relation to the momentum of the story and in relation to the development of the enactors of the story. Time, for the flicker of an eyelash, stands still, and one watches meaning swell and swell to a flood. The static moment serves to confront two characters with irreducible elements in each other, or one character with irreducible elements in himself, which once recognized, must cause a change of direction. The still moment leads to change, development, and movement.

Roderick goes on from that moment of "intellectual swoon" to a particular hill in Switzerland off which he falls. Milly finds that from that day in the park when she is "borne up for the hour" she is able to bear the steady sight of death. Maggie pieces together her conviction to her action and as she does so begins to propel the action rather than to be propelled by it. Strether finds himself in an altogether unforeseen course from that moment of the "perception of the man's identity"—Chad Newsome's, of course. His change of direction will transform not only his own, but Chad's world, too. There is a sense of consequence in James. Action induces reflection, reflection, further action.

And at the end of the story, there is a kind of resting in satisfaction, if not in completion. This is the way things are, the reader feels, and takes a breath; this is the way things turn out! There is a moment of revery, of reflection, of summarizing.

Roderick is dead at the conclusion of *Roderick Hudson*, but a comment made upon him lingers in the consciousness: "He had fallen from a great height, but he was singularly little disfigured." Milly Theale is dead also, at the end of *The Wings of the Dove*, but when she has been buried, and the two conspirators have gained their reward, the possession of the dead girl's money; they face each other and say, in awe of the shadow fallen upon them, "We shall never be again as we were!" Upon the final page of *The Golden Bowl*, the husband says to the wife, whom he had crassly neglected and flouted, and whom he had rediscovered, " 'See? I see nothing but *you*.' " The closing chord of emotion in *The Ambassadors* is that idea Strether has got hold of by changing his mind upon nearly all his preconceptions: " 'You'll be a brute you know—you'll be guilty of the last infamy—if you ever forsake her.' " This from the older man who had been sent out to rescue the younger man from the supposedly wicked arms of a Parisian mistress.

It is evident that the natural breath of the good story is the proper alternation (unforeseen and inevitable) of suspense and repose. But there are other zestful, unpredictable aspects of life which tempt the storyteller away from austere verities into the frivolity of melodrama. Its dangers are obvious: cheapness, sensationalism, shallowness.

What is to be done is to determine two points, for James has been occasionally called melodramatic: (1) To what extent is this so? and: (2) What does this quality, if it is melodrama, do to his fiction? Is it a help or a hindrance?

Upon the face of it, the melodramatic tendency seems present in the following categories: (*a*) excessive intervention; (*b*) unusual mystery; (*c*) coincidental or fortuitous occurrence; (*d*) instrumentation of a gross thing; (*e*) arbitrary violence.

These evidences of melodrama make their appearance through the good graces of the detective-story element, the ghost-story element, the thriller element, and the fairy-tale element. (But keep in the background the remembrance of the symbolical and metaphorical reference of these simplifying tendencies. Whereas one side of them is simple and tends to melodrama, the other side is simple and tends to value.)

Under category *a*, excessive intervention, are the extraordinary number of fairy godmothers or godfathers. To pick up one novel after another is to multiply cases. In the earliest novel, *Watch and Ward*, the relationship of the young man, Roger Lawrence, to the girl, Nora Lambert, is of the godfatherly type. She is an orphan of doubtful theatrical background, the daughter of a suicide; and he, with his proper, quiet, conscientious New England upbringing, decides to rescue her and make something of her.

Roderick Hudson in the novel which bears his name (*Roderick Hudson*, 1875) has a middle-aged, sophisticated, wealthy godfather in Rowland Mallet, who takes him from Northampton, Massachusetts, to study the art of sculpture in Italy. Isabel Archer in *The Portrait of a Lady* (1881) has the Touchetts, the mother, the father, and the son, each of whom tries to do something for her. In *The Princess Casamassima* (1886) Hyacinth Robinson, the poor apprentice, has his beautiful benefactress in Christina, the Princess, who is at first his dream of a great lady.

In *The Bostonians* (also published in 1886) Verena Tarrant, the Cinderella from the backwoods of charlatanry, has her fairy godmother of Beacon Street, Olive Chancellor. In *The Tragic Muse* (1890) Nick Dormer has Mr. Carteret and Miriam Rooth has Peter Sherringham. In *The Spoils of Poynton* (1896) Fleda Vetch has Mrs. Gereth, who takes her into Poynton, where every object is perfect and every emotion warped. In *The Awkward Age* (1899) Nanda Brookenham has Mr. Longdon, the old gentleman from the country. And in the last uncompleted novel, *The Ivory Tower* (published in 1917), James seemed to be writing another Cinderella story, with Graham Fielder as a young, male Cinderella to Mr. Betterman's serious, infinitely moneyed and portentous godfather.

James was conscious of using a naïve element. He had Newman in *The American* speak of his relation to Claire de Cintré as that of Beauty and the Beast. He had the narrator of *The Sacred Fount* say to one of the protagonists: "We're like the messengers and heralds in the tale of Cinderella, and I protest, I assure you, against any sacrifice of our dénouement. We've still the glass shoe to fit."

He had Nora Lambert, the orphan girl of *Watch and Ward*, say:

"I feel to-night like a princess in a fairy-tale. I am a poor creature, without a friend, without a penny or a home; and yet, here I sit by a blazing fire, with money, with food, with clothes, with love. The snow outside is burying the stone walls, and yet here I can sit and simply say, 'How pretty!' "

The suspense he created was in part the expectancy of the awakening of the sense of independence upon the part of each one of his endowed heroes and heroines. There is an inevitability of growth, development, and revolt with which the fairy godparent is incapable of dealing. James exhibited thus the very intractability of human nature. He showed it in the act of self-determination in the face of good fortune as well as bad.

The role of the sponsor is to pitch the hero into opportunities which are at the same time dangers and to stimulate the pulse of the story by the multiplication of choices. In common with other melodramatic aspects to be treated, this one gives freshness to the action. But for seriousness, for reality, the fairy godparent can only set the hero in motion; he cannot rescue him once he has gone his way and begun to choose and to accept or reject people and conditions. There are no last-minute reprieves at midnight. At that hour of crisis, the hero awakes to "the way things happen." He discovers reality and finds that he must outface fortune for himself. It is a definitely limited intervention, after all.

Category *b* is unusual mystery. The writer's fondness for the mysterious parent obviously belongs in this area of the melodramatic. Three cases come to mind: Christina Light in *Roderick Hudson,* Pansy Osmond in *The Portrait of a Lady,* and Hyacinth Robinson in *The Princess Casamassima.* In each novel the fact that each of these characters has an unknown, a hidden parent, belongs to the naïve, zestful, melodramatic side of the writer's temperament. But also, and this is the way in which James makes melodrama subordinate to another value, in each case the discovery of the parent means the breaking down of a dream into a wicked reality. It is a fairy tale played out of key.

James was as fond of the search after the thing hid as the person hid. This accounts for the important place that a kind of detective-story element has in his work. What he did was to ally the breathless sort of interest possible in the pure puzzle of the popular detective-story fiction to a subtle search for motives. Lambert Strether's worried hunt in *The Ambassadors* for the reality and truth of Chad Newsome's motives through false scents and in and out of dead ends and misleading side paths is the sublimation of the hunt for the clue. The clue becomes the motive. The freshness and unexpectedness of each disclosure owes something to the skill of the lower form of storytelling.

James had a love of mysteriousness for its own sake. But he was able to harness it. There are the ghost stories, and there is, for instance, the symbolic puzzle of such a story as *The Figure in the Carpet,* whose meaning is coincident with the unanswerableness of life. Or, working with the elements of the mystery story, he achieved such a novel as *The Sacred Fount.* In it, the narrator is a detector of hidden emotional states. His game, almost unhinging his own mind, is to deduce motivation from the overt action of the two very clever, very dangerous manipulators of other human beings.

The ghostly and the ghastly ambiguous owe their effective appearance to the author's use of vivid and possibly melodramatic techniques. The aim is the intimation to the reader that there are horrors and uglinesses in life which cannot be explained. The desire is to open the crack, for shock value, suddenly at the reader's own feet. But for effectiveness, the yawning of the moral abyss must be unexpected. The method of achieving shock value avails itself here too of the methods of fiction less conscientious of motive than his.

But note two points: his characters are more interesting just because they live on the edge of abysses; and the narration is not hurt by the sharp intake of breath forced upon the reader by the means used. And James did not throw away the advantage of this touch of melodrama by playing with it in a void. He always allied the ghostly horrible to a normal or common-sense base of action or character.

Owen Wingrave, in the story of that name, is struck dead by a ghost, but the author leads one to that horrific conclusion from a reasonable account of Owen's difficulties: his desire to skip the military training which was a tradition with his family; his unsuccessful struggle with the family and the sweetheart who accused him of cowardice; his vigil in the haunted room (to prove his bravery); and his death by the ghost of the room, a *military* ancestor. The family wins; the obvious victory, only, is ghostly. The author said concerning this and other ghost stories that it was "the note I wanted; that of the strange and sinister embroidered on the very type of the normal and easy."

The character of the governess in *The Turn of the Screw* has just the right note of limited common sense and propriety to furnish the necessary foil to the other and unnatural note of impropriety and horror in Miss Jessel, Peter Quint, Flora, and little Miles. Elaborate psychoanalysis of the governess would turn her into a creature who spoils the point of the story. And we have James' own word for the way to take her. To H. G. Wells, in 1898, he wrote as follows on this interesting point:

The grotesque business I had to make her picture and the childish psychology I had to make her trace and present, were, for me at least, a very difficult job, in which absolute lucidity and logic, a singleness of effect, were imperative. Therefore I had to rule out subjective complications on her own—play of tone etc.; and keep her impersonal save for the most obvious and indispensable little note of neatness, firmness and courage—without which she wouldn't have had her data.

Category *c* is coincidental or fortuitous occurrence. Roderick's death in *Roderick Hudson,* to cite a case, is unnecessary, and so also is the fire which at the end of *The Spoils of Poynton* destroys the house and all the spoils within it. But both events are grateful to the sense of the way things *ought* to happen. The coincidence of the close association of the two stepparents in *What Maisie Knew* is an issue to boggle at. But in the interest of the tangle which ensues between Maisie's real parents (divorced) and her stepparents, who take an extramarital interest in each other, interest wins over plausibility. In this case the unlikeliness is smothered or forgotten.

As noted before, the implausible is too strong for one novel at least, *The American,* and partly spoils its effectiveness. But wherever inconsequence, coincidence, and the frivolousness of chance seem incidental, they serve the writer well and remind the reader that life is indeed chancy and made up of inconsequence, coincidence, and frivolity.

The boldness of the unforeseen occasion, the daring of the unexpected meeting, the suddenness of the disclosure of a secret, all evidences of melodrama, have in part a serious reference to James' sincere notion of fate. This is his only cosmology (at least in his fiction). Things will turn out so! Why not help them to turn out so?

Category *d* in this telling over of melodramatic aspects is the instrumentation of a gross or material object in the fate of his characters. One thinks of the letter in *The American* with which Newman can break the Bellegardes; of the cracked, gold-plated crystal bowl in *The Golden Bowl;* of the "ivory tower" in the novel of that name; of the picture in *The Sense of the Past.* But here one is almost out of the sphere of melodrama. The person in the story, Newman, Maggie Verver, Graham Fielder, or Ralph Pendrel, is already predisposed to a certain action before the fateful object makes its appearance. The action is character determined, but the object is the occasion for action and is of good use in dramatizing the action taken.

There is a surprising amount of violent action for a reflective author in the full course of James' novels and tales. This is category *e*, under melodrama. There are suicides in the novels *Watch and Ward* and *The Princess Casamassima,* and in the stories *The Patagonia, The Modern Warning,* and *A Round of Visits.* Daisy Miller's death may be said to have occurred through willful negligence, and Dolcino's in *The Author of Beltraffio* is a negative kind of murder. The deaths of Owen Wingrave in the story bearing his name and of Miles in *The Turn of the Screw* and of Louisa Chantry in *The Visits* are unnatural. Juliana, old as she is, in *The Aspern Papers,* dies of shock; Morgan Moreen, "the pupil," of the willful aggravation of his family. Sir A. B. C. Beadel-Muffet's supposed death in *The Papers* turns that story at a strategic point from broad satire to a satirical thriller. Roderick Hudson's death, if accidental, is certainly violent. The fire in *The Spoils of Poynton,* mentioned before, is unnecessary but gratifying. The bodily scuffle over Verena Tarrant at the end of *The Bostonians* is an undignified but effective brawl.

One purpose which the display of violence serves is to give a satisfying, sensuous shape to the brooding, internal differences of the characters. The physical action gives an objective show of the idea. Thus violence serves to vivify character. As for its effect on the narration, the forward drive of action, it gives relief and a full stop for emphasis.

Sometimes James miscalculated. Agatha Grice's death in *A Modern Warning* (she kills herself because her English husband hates her country, America, and publishes a vicious book expressing his views) does not have a sufficient preparation. The most convincing circumstance of her distraction, a morbid love for a brother who is an England-hater, is not sufficiently stressed.

In most of his instances of brutal and violent action, the intensity of the emotion, as it is expressed in action, serves him well. The violent act is a judgment upon the customary and usual tenor of existence and momentarily sheds a fierce light upon it.

Melodrama then transcends its own ordinary purposes of excitement and shock and color. It transports the reader by those gifts into another sphere of concentration and value. Since melodrama is a recessive trait in James, and not a dominant one, it serves him well. It acts to enhance complicated meanings with vivid enactments. And it is an effective contrast to his dominant mode.

James is oblique, he is indirect, he is difficult. But he is not difficult for nothing. There are two kinds of fruitless complexity: that of the worker who fails to understand himself and his problem and involves himself in helpless entanglements and that of the worker who has a shallow pride in inventing and multiplying pointless involvements. James' kind of complexity was, on the contrary, an effort of the mind to bring about a real and fruitful order. The means, if difficult, if complex, seen in relation to the end, accomplish their purpose. They mark the real complexity of real living.

This is his "crooked corridor." This is the stumbling block to a just understanding of James. He once said soberly that "the long journey round about the truth no more than served me right; just as after all it at last left me quite content." The difficulty is the condition of the journeying, but the magnet is the truth. The "crooked corridor" leads at last to the "Presence."

These phrases occur in an important letter James wrote in 1899 to Mrs. Humphry Ward. The passage reads in part as follows:

> Your material suffers a little from the fact that the reader feels you approach your subject too *immediately,* show him its elements, the cards in your hand, too bang off from the first page—so that a wait to begin to guess *what and whom the thing is going to be about* doesn't impose itself: the ante-chamber or two and the crooked corridor before he is already in the Presence. The other (objection) is that you don't give him a positive sense of dealing with your subject from its logical centre.

Results bear him out. His stories and novels have the honor to live in the mind with the forcefulness of the single impression. To appreciate James with justice, however, one should undergo some of his labor, one should trace the working of certain of the difficult means. One should follow the "corridor" to its destination, which James called the "logical centre."

All the means of art are restrictive forces. The writer cannot do his job just any way. He must always do it some particular way. What this truth leads one to consider, then, as something not to be got around is the artist's conscience. As regards the work to be done (the novel or short story to be completed), it should be of an absolute severity. At least this was James' view.

The first of the restrictive means in which James exercised his art was the "point of view." There are two areas in which the "point of view" operates: outside the story, in the mind of the creator; and inside the story. James discussed the second area particularly.

But one can trace the "point of view" back even into the creator's unconscious mind and see that it works there, too, to form his general focus and his particular idiosyncrasies. Innate character, for instance, caused James to see "a psychological reason [as] an object adorably pictorial," and to write as one who did so see. It caused him to write about "handlers of the fiddle-string and the fumblers for the essence" in preference to "the mainly 'broad' and monotonously massive characters." (The quotation is a reaction to Stevenson's Lord Hermiston.) This choice of the kind of character he handled, James was wise enough to see, was a limitation imposed upon him by his temperament. He could have little control over it.

But consider next the "point of view" of the creator as he handles his raw material—already thrust upon him by his temperament. His salvation, as James saw it, was just the limitation which he put upon himself. He said that "the novelist is a particular window," and he practiced his belief.

His premise for good work was limitation. But it was limitation self-imposed. He saw that the writer was subject to as many delightful and dangerous choices as he demonstrated to be true of his characters. The dangerous multiplicity of choice and the hard necessity of choosing together made up the honorable condition of living. A quotation from the Preface to *The Portrait of a Lady* states the matter in a metaphor reminiscent of the one quoted above:

> The house of fiction has in short not one window, but a million
> . . . at each of them stands a figure with a pair of eyes, or at least
> with a field-glass, which forms, again and again, for observation, a
> unique instrument, insuring to the person making use of it an im-
> pression distinct from every other. He and his neighbors are watching
> the same show, but one seeing more where the other sees less, one
> seeing black where the other sees white, one seeing big where the
> other sees small, one seeing coarse where the other sees fine. . . .
> The spreading field, the human scene, is the "choice of subject"; the
> pierced aperture, either broad or balconied or split-like and low-
> browed, is the "literary form"; but they are, singly or together, as
> nothing without the posted presence of the watcher—without, in
> other words, the consciousness of the artist. Tell me what the artist is,
> and I will tell you of what he has *been* conscious. Thereby I shall
> express to you at once his boundless freedom and his "moral" refer-
> ence.

Further, he declared his adherence to the principle in question with the vivacity of expression of the true believer: "What
I have said about the 'rule' of presentation being, in each
case, hard and fast, *that* I will go the stake and burn with a
slow fire for—and the slowest that will burn at all."

This emotion is a great strength in his writing. For he loved
the way as well as the end. He believed in the rules he set up
for himself not only with the mind, but with the heart. Their
operation in his works was passionate. There was no break in
his temperament between the way things ought to be done and
the way they were done—only the difficulty. And that difficulty
was insoluble; perfection impossible; and the natural condition
of the artist's life was the struggle to do what could not be done.

Each book, then, to the genuine artist, to be worth doing,
must have an inherent order. The idea of that order which lives
in his imagination is his "point of view" toward the work in
process. The writing of the piece of fiction consists of the choice,
arrangement, and elimination of such facts as he sees in the
natural world. But the facts of the world assault the mind too
densely for sense. They are too tightly packed, too higgledy-
piggledy, for ideas to move through them. Art makes the large

assumption that sense is there, but that the facts must be arranged for sense, which is truth, to show through. And in writing any particular book, the writer must have a particular narrative interest and a particular psychological interest. Or so thought James, and acted as he thought.

All the books in some way pay tribute to the central idea of his career, the problem of the individual person in the organized world. There is in them differentiation and multiplication of the occasion of this theme. And each book is, besides and in itself, a particular version of the idea.

In *The Portrait of a Lady* the idea, perhaps, is that of individual freedom, its opportunities and its dangers. The strictly limited means of working out the idea are all contained in the observation of Isabel Archer's marriage. The idea of *The Bostonians* might possibly be stated as the sovereignty and independence of art; its telling is limited to a small and special world, that of Bostonian reform; and its development must work itself out entirely in the struggle between Olive Chancellor, reformer, and Basil Ransom, reactionary, over the person of Verena Tarrant, who, if she represents the divine principle of art, is also a flighty, impressionable young girl of doubtful background. The idea of *The Ambassadors* seems to be the discovery by a middle-aged, imaginative American man of letters that there is something to be said for enjoyment as well as duty. But the presentation of the theme is implicit, never explicit, in the story of Lambert Strether's relationship to Chad Newsome.

James held to it that if one tells a story, one should tell it in a fitting manner. Thinness did not result from this severity. Relevant details were endless. It was for the further ordering of the relevant parts of the whole that James developed the element which he himself named as the "point of view." The "point of view" in this sense is simply the logic of the consciousness exhibited inside the story. It is not necessarily the same logic from one story to another, but it is necessary that one method be chosen for each story, and then that method be held to for the honor of the maker.

In two of the early novels, *Washington Square* and *The Europeans,* there is no strict "point of view." James wrote these novels before he had impressed himself with his own law. However, two other early novels, *Roderick Hudson* and *The Ameri-can*, do hold with a more or less strict adherence to the rule. In the first, Rowland Mallet is the eye of the reader; in the second, "the American" is.

The Portrait of a Lady, which came later than the books mentioned above, has not one single "point of view," it is true; but the shift of viewpoint in it, upon examination, proves to be deliberate, and a part of the pattern. Here the reader sees a good early example of the law: the "point of view" as a decisive element of the structure.

In this novel there is, first, a brief, introductory section in which Isabel Archer, around whom the entire book is built, is anticipated; and the consciousness of the situation is a joint one shared among the three men awaiting her: old Mr. Touchett, his son Ralph, and Lord Warburton. Next, Isabel enters; her consciousness, her "point of view" becomes the sole receptor of the action; through her the reader sees all that is permitted to him to see.

The sudden shift of the "point of view" at the halfway mark of the novel, from Isabel's to Osmond's and Madame Merle's "point of view," causes a perceptible drop in the temperature. The change in viewpoint is dramatic and dynamic, a part of the emotional structure of the book.

Before that moment the reader had gone along with Isabel, knowing only what she knows, even if suspecting more. This turnabout of viewpoint serves to confirm the suspicion that Isabel has been deceived in her future husband. For the time, the reader is a participator in Osmond's schemes. Then that vista shuts down.

The reader is again with Isabel, but this time with a knowledge superior to hers. The time is a year after her marriage to Osmond. Her mind opens only gradually to the reader. A part of the suspense from this point thereon is to make out how much Isabel has discovered of Osmond's character during the twelve months of her marriage. It is only in her midnight soliloquy at a point three-fourths of the way through the novel that the reader is entirely at one with Isabel's most private thoughts. With her, then, one stays to the end. The "point of view," as it can be seen, had been used constructively. It is the principal way, in this novel, that James makes the reader understand trust and understand betrayal.

James set himself harder tasks and used more limiting "points of view" as he continued to write novel after novel and to feel more and more the fascination of the difficult. *What Maisie Knew*, for instance, is an ugly tangle of lusts and hates seen entirely through the eyes of the child who is the immediate occasion and excuse for the struggle. The writer allowed himself no shift of viewpoint here, but worked his way to a difficult solution with Maisie's mind as his only focus. He was rewarded by the interesting emotional combination, innocence contemplating depravity. *The Ambassadors*, too, is a case of the single consciousness, Lambert Strether's alone, which sees and reacts to all that happens not only to him, but to Chad, Marie de Vionnet, and all the Pococks.

While James did not seem to think that the single "point of view" was the one supreme way of telling a story, he must have been conscious of an effect which it had in reinforcing the idea, present in all his stories, of the loneliness of the single human person. He enforced that sense of moral loneliness upon the reader more effectively by making him undergo solitude with the character possessed of the sentient consciousness.

The Awkward Age develops in a different manner, in a series of shifts of emphasis from one character to another: Mr. Longdon, Van, Mrs. Brook, the Duchess, Mitchy, and so on. All, however, one after the other, concentrate their attention upon the one center of interest, Nanda Brookenham's youthful exposure to the corruption of her mother's interesting circle. All consider in turn the effect of that exposure and decide according to character whether that exposure makes Nanda good or bad. The strange thing, hardly apparent to one at first, is that in this story James was not using the "point of view" at all. He was able to get at these people by another means, to be discussed below.

In *The Tragic Muse* the "logical centre" is the person of the actress Miriam Rooth. Her personality, her life, her art attract the attention of various characters, two of whom, Nick Dormer and Peter Sherringham, share between them the "point of view" of the novel. *The Golden Bowl* was a second try at the kind of shift in the "point of view" done earlier in *The Portrait of a Lady.* Book I, "The Prince," focuses upon the husband; Book II, "The Princess," upon the wife. The shift in the "point of view" is accompanied by a massive shift in emotion. Book I is a building up of a complication and tension; Book II, a liberation. The two halves of the action are hinged together by the intermediary consciousness of Fanny Assingham, who has involved herself in both camps and shares the confidences of both the husband and the wife.

What is to be remembered in noting these differences in the use of the "point of view" is that the variation is deliberate; that it is manifold in its patterns; that it shapes emotion as well as pattern; and that the limitation placed upon the means of expression makes for a greater force of expression. Composition holds life. It does not let the vital heat escape. I paraphrase James: "Form alone *takes,* and holds and preserves, substance—" Caught forever in the particular shape of the narrative, the color and high pitch of life endure.

As James came to see the importance of the "point of view," he was faced with kindred problems: How far was he to "go behind" his characters? How far was he to treat them by scenic presentation? He saw again that variety of method satisfied him better than rigidity, but that in the case of each book, a particular method must hold good.

Both the "going behind" and the telling the story in scenes work for the same end, to give the bystander (the reader) insight into the secret and vital life of his people. The "going behind" allowed him scope for psychological analysis; scenic presentation gave him scope for revealing action. He admitted his own deviations and admitted his content with deviation in a letter of the year 1899, already quoted in part above:

I "go behind" right and left in "The Princess Casamassima," "The Bostonians," "The Tragic Muse," just as I do the same but singly in "The American," and "Maisie," and just as I do it consistently *never at all* (save for a false and limited *appearance,* here and there, of doing it a *little,* which I haven't time to explain) in "The Awkward Age."

It is interesting to note that the three novels mentioned by James as ones in which he was content to "go behind" right and left are his realistic, broad novels of the middle part of his career. Not one of them contains the strict and single "point of view." The eyes which see and describe the action are anonymous and see beyond the range of vision possible to any one character taking part in that action.

This fact allows a looser, broader, more traditional mode of presentation. Things and persons appear in a hard, clear, definite light. The analysis of personality is as much a matter of picture as of discrimination of motive. The senses and the intellect are rewarded simultaneously.

The following descriptions, in which one can see James "going behind," are from *The Bostonians:*

Basil Ransom

This lean, pale, sallow, shabby, striking young man, with his superior head, his sedentary shoulders, his expression of bright grimness and hard enthusiasm, his provincial, distinguished appearance . . . the reader who likes a complete image, who desires to read with the senses as well as with the reason, is entreated not to forget that he prolonged his consonants and swallowed his vowels, that he was guilty of elisions and interpolations which were equally unexpected, and that his discourse was pervaded by something sultry and vast, something almost African in its rich, basking tone, something that suggested the teeming expanse of the cottonfield.

Olive Chancellor

She was habited in a plain dark dress, without any ornaments, and her smooth, colourless hair was confined . . . this pale girl, with her light-green eyes, her pointed features and nervous manner, was visibly morbid; it was as plain as day that she was morbid.

Miss Birdseye

She was a little old lady, with an enormous head; that was the first thing Ransom noticed—the vast, fair, protuberant, candid, ungarnished brow, surmounting a pair of weak, kind, tired-looking eyes, and ineffectually balanced in the rear by a cap which had the air of falling backward, and which Miss Birdseye suddenly felt for while she talked, with unsuccessful irrelevant movements. She had a sad, soft, pale face, which (and it was the effect of her whole head) looked as if it had been soaked, blurred, and made vague by exposure to some slow dissolvent. The long practice of philanthropy had not given accent to her features; it had rubbed out their transitions, their meanings. The waves of sympathy, of enthusiasm, had wrought upon them in the same way in which the waves of time finally modify the surface of old marble busts, gradually washing away their sharpness, their details.

The Tragic Muse is more consistent in its manner of presentation than *The Bostonians,* with which it shares a bustle and broadness not found before or after. As noted above in the discussion of the book's "point of view," Miriam Rooth is the center of gravity of the novel. She lives in the minds of other characters; he does not "go behind" her, yet she lives more largely and more heroically than any of the others.

Of the three novels cited above as realistic and traditional, *The Princess Casamassima* has the least of this "going behind." After the childhood and youth of his hero, Hyacinth Robinson, is past, the writer allowed Hyacinth himself to be the eyes of the novel. And just as his interests alone are thereafter the only interests presented to the reader, he is the only character whom James "goes behind" to any extent, that is, after Hyacinth is of age.

It has been noted that in *The American* and in *What Maisie Knew* James held to the single "point of view." The allied technique was to "go behind" but to "go behind" only the possessors of the viewpoint. His aim was to cause the reader to identify himself with that character. His method was to cause that reader to take part in the thoughts and emotions of the principal as they occurred, and to share his hope or his fear, his suspense or his relief, as the case might be.

What he did, on the other hand, in *The Awkward Age* was to reach the same place, the same end—live people, vital action —by the opposite means. He did not, in this novel, permit a special intimacy to develop between the reader and one or more characters. He used techniques of the stage here. He had been unsuccessful, or at least thought himself unsuccessful, as a playwright, but the playwright's means served him well in this and many of the other novels.

The Awkward Age is an extreme experiment in scenic presentation. It is his most difficult novel, but taken on its own terms, an absolute success. He "goes behind" none of the char-

acters. Its people: Nanda Brookenham and her formidable
mother with the "hanging head of a broken lily," Van of "the
sacred terror," ugly Mitchy, the Duchess and her little Aggie,
Mr. Longdon, Lord Petherton, and the others appear as if upon
a stage. They speak, they act, and all that the innocent bystander—the reader—knows comes to him through these, as
it were, public actions. (There have to be at least two characters together, at a time, for the flint of contact to make the display required.) Yet James was able, through the exhibition of
overt action, to convey not only the brilliant surface of Mrs.
Brook's bad world, but, as if by magic, its secret depths, as well.

To illustrate the revelations possible in one chapter by the
oblique method, here are those of the first: (*a*) that Van has an
ambiguous relationship with Mrs. Brook; (*b*) that Van thinks
the two young girls, Nanda and Aggie, possible choices for the
honor of being Van's wife; (*c*) that Van thinks Nanda more
charming; (*d*) that the tone of Mrs. Brook's circle is fast; (*e*) that
Mrs. Brook is sorry to have a daughter as old as Nanda; (*f*) that
Mr. Longdon, fresh from the country, is going to be an interested observer of Mrs. Brook's fast circle.

The theme, as in all his stories, is simple: What is virtue?
For Aggie, protected and ignorant, virtue is all outside her; for
Nanda, virtue is all inside her, and none outside. The watching and judging of Nanda as she grows into a personality in
this circle constitute the action. The reader is as if caught and
constrained and made helpless by interest. The pressures put
upon his attention resemble the cruel constraints put upon
Nanda's development in her twisted world.

I have used those novels which James himself mentioned as
good examples. But the care for method and the care for variety
in method could be pointed out in the other novels. *The Sacred
Fount* and *The Spoils of Poynton* both exhibit the single "point
of view." In one, James "goes behind" his narrator; in the other,
he does not.

On the other hand, the last unfinished book, *The Ivory
Tower*, is not an example of purity of method. It is neither a
story of a single "point of view" nor one of strict scenic presentation. It shifts unmistakably and of a purpose from the focal consciousness of Rosanna Gaw to that of Graham Fielder, and

then presents Cissie Foy and Horton Vint without exploring their thoughts except as they give themselves away by word and deed. It is a mixture, but even in its unfinished state it is apparent that James intended to preserve a balance between the thoughts of Rosanna and the thoughts of Graham.

Whatever means James used to present character, he had it upon his conscience to objectify all the parts. What he intended in writing each novel was the rounding out of an independent, self-supporting world with a life of its own. He could not intrude his own, his writer's consciousness, into that world without breaching a wall and destroying that world's sovereignty.

Therefore the "I" in any story is not Henry James, not even Henry James disguised. The "I" is a person in the story, as are also the "he" and "she" with the important, developing "point of view." He thought the novel had to be alive in all its parts and could not be so if the teller of the story came in from the outside and postured and grimaced and used the story as an excuse to advance his personal aims. There is, in fact, only one *novel* told in the first person: *The Sacred Fount.*

This is James' antiexpressive, antiexpansive credo. His activity was all a creation of form which in its own shape might well mean what was in him, but whose obvious connections with his personal ego had been broken in the process of creation. A novel or a story was never an excuse for James to say something or be something; it was not a subjective opportunity. The novel was a *thing* which he had made or tried to make complete and perfect in itself. Therefore his work was nonreforming and nonedifying. To say this is not to deny the books substance. No insight which he had ever gained was wasted. It was transformed and built into the structure of the book. And perhaps just because his truth was a nonegotistic truth, it lives more securely and endures longer than partial and subjective truths.

Like paint to the painter, musical notes to the composer, concrete and steel to the architect, words are what the writer works with in order to build. Language is the sensuous sea in which both meaning and manner float. It sluices action and the emotions and thoughts of his characters with an embracing amplitude of sympathy and sensibility.

The obvious first point to set down about James' use of language is that it was a means which developed from the simple to the complex. Illustrations abound.

The early style shows well in a description of an old, dead New York in the story *Georgina's Reasons*, written just after the Civil War:

This little drama went on, in New York, in the ancient days, when Twelfth Street had but lately ceased to be suburban, when the squares had wooden palings, which were not often painted, when there were poplars in important thoroughfares and pigs in the lateral ways, when the theatres were miles distant from Madison Square, and the battered rotunda of Castle Garden echoed with expensive vocal music, when "the park" meant the grass-plats of the City Hall, and the Bloomingdale Road was an eligible drive, when Hoboken, of a summer afternoon, was a genteel resort, and the handsomest house in town was on the corner of Fifth Avenue and Fifteenth Street.

There is a brisk sort of music here in the lilt of the short, neat phrase. But compare this with the more relaxed rhythm of a descriptive passage from *The Bostonians* (1886). This is Marmion, a Bostonian holiday place where Olive Chancellor had taken Verena Tarrant in an attempt to get her to fall out of love with the southerner, Basil Ransom:

The little straggling, loosely-clustered town lay along the edge of a blue inlet, on the other side of which was a low, wooded shore, with a gleam of white sand where it touched the water. The narrow bay carried the vision outward to a picture that seemed at once bright and dim—a shining, slumbering summer-sea, and a far-off, circling line of coast, which, under the August sun, was hazy and delicate. . . . It was a town where you smelt the breath of the hay in the streets and you might gather blackberries in the principal square. The houses looked at each other across the grass—low, rusty, crooked, distended houses, with dry, cracked faces and the dim eyes of small-paned, stiffly-sliding windows. Their little door-yards bristled with rank, old-fashioned flowers, mostly yellow; and on the quarter that stood back from the sea the fields sloped upward, and the woods in which they presently lost themselves looked down over the roofs.

There were certain afternoons in August, long beautiful and terrible, when one felt that the summer was rounding its curve, and the rustle of the full-leaved trees in the slanting golden light, in the breeze that ought to be delicious, seemed the voice of the coming autumn, of the warnings and dangers of life—portentous, insufferable hours.

Maturity had brought both accuracy of vision and openness to feeling. The expression of the physical scene and of the related mood is as yet straightforward.

The later, richer development brought with it difficulty, for every part was somehow involved in every other part of the whole. Yet it brought fullness and completeness too. For the description of the sea storm in Venice in *The Wings of the Dove* is the description of Densher's moral despair. The details are the real details of the physical scene, but they are completely swayed by the particular, rich attitude of despair held by the one who experienced the storm:

> It was a Venice all of evil that had broken out . . . a Venice of cold, lashing rain from a low black sky, of wicked wind raging through long narrow passes, of general arrest and interruption, with people engaged in all the water-life huddled, stranded and wageless, bored and cynical, under archways and bridges. . . . The wet and the cold were now to reckon with, and it was precisely, to Densher, as if he had seen the obliteration, at a stroke, of the margin on a faith in which they were all living. The margin had been his name for it —for the thing that, though it had held out, could bear no shock. The shock, in some form, had come, and he wondered about it while, threading his way among loungers as vague as himself, he dropped his eyes sightlessly on the rubbish in the shops.

The greater complication of words is at one with the greater complication of meaning. From the callous, competent efficiency of youth, he had grown into a larger, more feeling, more suffering sufficiency of fruition. The end of the career shows one a man with sharpened, delicate tools, almost in a humble despair over the multiplicity of shapes to be carved.

The next obvious point to consider is that the man who tried the difficult way would fall into excesses and extravagances. He could greatly and famously overuse the adverb; he could pile circumlocution upon circumlocution; he could, in the difficulty of tracking down an obscure meaning, lose himself in the dark. What should be well remembered is the fact that his faults were those of generosity and not of parsimony. What James was trying ceaselessly to express was the almost inexpressible. His important effort was to bring into the novel the curious mixture which he found in life of good and bad, high and low, dark and bright. He dared to encompass the scale; he dared to be grand. His faults, after all, become him.

And his language, even when stretched beyond acceptability, is a personal voice. It is his own, and once heard, can never be forgotten. When right, when just, it is capable of wit, of eloquence, and of power. Such is the effect of the conclusion of *The Beast in the Jungle:*

> One's doom, however, was never baffled. . . . The Beast had lurked indeed, and the Beast, at its hour, had sprung. . . . He had justified his fear and achieved his fate; he had failed, with the last exactitude, of all he was to fail of. . . . This horror of waking—*this* was knowledge, knowledge under the breath of which the very tears in his eyes seemed to freeze. Through them, none the less, he tried to fix and hold it; he kept it there before him so that he might feel the pain. That at least, belated and bitter, had something of the taste of life. But the bitterness suddenly sickened him, and it was as if, horribly, he saw, in the truth, in the cruelty of his image, what had been appointed and done. He saw the Jungle of his life and saw the lurking Beast; then, while he looked, perceived it, as by a stir of the air, rise, huge and hideous, for the leap that was to settle him. His eyes darkened—it was close; and, instinctively turning, in his hallucination, to avoid it, he flung himself, face down, on the tomb.

His language is a fine glove upon the hand of action, or of that thought which in his books is action.

It will be seen in retrospect that the examples of description given above are not pure. With the possible exception of the first, they are active; they reveal thought; they impel movement.

In the same way, dialogue (another use he made of language) shows itself to belong to the whole. A customary objection to James is that the talk in his novels is not natural. Of course not. His people talk more brilliantly than is normal, and they say more of what they think. This talk has an edge to it; it cuts and slices its way through the dull crust of the ordinary to the living center of "the way things happen." Conversation in these stories is functional, not decorative.

In a passage in *Roderick Hudson,* Rowland Mallet had been

remonstrating with the young artist for his bad treatment of his mother and Mary Garland, his fiancée, who had come abroad from New England to be with him in Rome. The truth comes out, in talk, with abrupt and ugly directness:

"They bore me to death," Roderick went on. . . .
"Miserable boy!" Rowland groaned. "They're the most touching, most amiable of women."
"Very likely. But they mean no more to me than a piano means to a pig."
"I can say this," said Rowland in a moment. "I don't pretend to understand the state of your relations with Miss Garland."
Roderick shrugged his shoulders and let his hands drop at his sides. "She thinks all the world of me. She likes me as if I were good to eat. She's saving me up, cannibal-fashion, as if I were a big feast. That's the state of my relations." He smiled strangely.
"Have you broken off your engagement?"
"Broken it off? You can't break off a star in Orion. You can only," Roderick explained, "let it alone."

In *The Wings of the Dove* the shock of Kate Croy's full intention for herself and for him breaks upon Merton Densher as they talk. She had persuaded him to hide the fact of their engagement from Milly Theale, to please Milly, and to let Milly like him. Densher, who had been pitifully bemused by Kate, learns at last what he has been doing and what he is to do now:

"Since she's to die I'm to marry her, . . . so that when her death has taken place I shall in the natural course have money?"

And Kate answers:

"You'll in the natural course have money. We shall in the natural course be free."
"Oh, oh, oh!" Densher softly murmured.
"Yes, yes, yes."

In *The Golden Bowl* it is the erring Prince, speaking to his wife, who has the last words: on Charlotte, who had ceased to distract him, " 'She's stupid' "; on everything, " 'Everything's terrible, cara, in the heart of man' "; and on Maggie, " 'See? I see nothing but *you*.' "
Conversation, in James' stories, it should be admitted, is more

extreme than in real life. His people say what they mean and they say it with a vividness which is artificial as all art is artificial. Talk of such kind has a cruel clarity. It cleanses and calms the spirit by its honesty. Dialogue is an effective part of the structure.

It is to this truth, the importance of structure, that anyone who reads James with care returns again and again. What beauty there is in him, what poetry, what truth, are all welded into structure. All the means together, the basic ones of narration, the dubious ones of melodrama, the specialized ones of the "point of view," "going behind," the telling of the story in scenes, the objectifying, the use of words, all contribute to the structure, or rather, as he thought of it, the living organism.

For this concern is the heart of the matter, what he really cared for. Late in life, he wrote a magnanimous letter to H. G. Wells, in regard to that writer's parody of him in *Boon*. In *Boon* he had met once more the shock of misunderstanding and misreading. This time the jeers had come from a writer to whom he had been sympathetic and perhaps overgenerous.

His words, with their proper ring of pride, their reserve, their dignity, and their due appraisal of his own way of doing, speak better than any critic's the justification of the work:

I have more or less mastered your appreciation of H. J. which I have found very curious and interesting after a fashion—though it has naturally not filled me with a fond elation. It is difficult of course for a writer to put himself *fully* in the place of another writer who finds him extraordinarily futile and void, and who is moved to publish that to the world . . . one *has* to fall back upon one's sense of one's good parts. . . . For I should otherwise seem to forget what it is that my poetic and my appeal to experience rest upon. They rest upon *my* measure of fulness—fulness of life and of the projection of it, which seems to you such an emptiness of both. I don't mean to say I don't wish I could do twenty things I can't—many of which you do so livingly; but I confess I ask myself what would become in that case of some of those to which I am most addicted and by which interest seems to me most beautifully producible. I hold that interest may be, *must* be, exquisitely made and created, and that if we don't make it, we who undertake to, nobody and nothing will make it for us; . . . It is art that *makes* life, makes interest, makes importance, for our consideration and application of these things, and I know of no substitute whatever for the force and beauty of its process. If I were Boon I should say that any pretence of such a substitute is helpless and hopeless humbug; but I wouldn't be Boon for the world, and am only yours faithfully . . .

This statement to one in the camp of the enemy is a characteristic affirmation of James' belief in the unity of the living and the making. There could be no art without life, no life without art. The welding together of the two was the faith in which he lived and died.

PART Seven

The House of Life
and the Palace of Art

WHEN WILLIAM AND HENRY JAMES WERE SMALL BOYS LIVing for a time in the Paris of Louis Napoleon, they were accustomed to take almost daily walks through the busy city streets to the Luxembourg or to the Louvre. There William would attempt to copy his favorite pictures, and Henry would watch. Together, solemnly, at thirteen and twelve, they would pass judgment upon and admire, sometimes the good, sometimes the bad, pictures of the 1850's.

The expedition to the museum became a customary habit, and the Louvre a place to which Henry returned again and again, often alone. The busy streets outside, along the river; the halls inside, thronged almost as the streets were; and, above all, the profusion of the pictures, the good and the bad, came to mean a great deal to the boy.

It was only the articulate old man, looking back at himself, the serious small boy of a lost past, who could find the words to characterize the experience. The habit was a likely enough occupation for a lonely, foreign boy in a strange city. But the words which the old man used to evoke the memory have the effect of magnification and transformation. The disproportion between the occasion and the reaction is remarkable but in character. This is Henry James, himself.

Upon his first visit the child had hung back; he had been "appalled but uplifted." This was not just a visit to a museum, this was a crisis. It was "that instant as if the hour had struck from a clock. . . ." He did not just *see* the pictures with his young, appalled eyes, he *heard* them: "It was as if they had gathered there into a vast deafening chorus; I shall never forget how—speaking, that is, for my own sense—they filled those vast halls with the influence rather of some complicated sound, diffused and reverberant, than of such visibilities as one could directly deal with."

The scene was "a vast bright gage"; and the Galerie d'Apollon, in particular, was not just a roomful of pictures, but a "bridge over to Style." The air was not dusty, museum air; what he inhaled was "a general sense of *glory*." The sensations which he experienced were at least of the type of "a love-philtre or fear-philtre."

Memory had enriched the scene too. Time and experience and the morbidity of genius had worked together to form something extraordinary when he came to write down this incident of a long gone past. For an older James had dreamed an unforgettable dream, fixed significantly in that same Galerie d'Apollon where he had stepped as on a bridge over into the world of Style and Form. The dream, adding another dimension to the whole, was of

the sudden pursuit, through an open door, along a huge high saloon, of a just dimly-described figure that retreated in terror before my rush and dash (a glare of inspired reaction from irresistible but shameful dread), out of the room I had a moment before been desperately, and all the more abjectly, defending by the push of my shoulder against hard pressure on lock and bar from the other side. The lucidity, not to say the sublimity, of the crisis had consisted of the great thought that I, in my appalled state, was probably still more appalling than the awful agent, creature or presence, whatever he was, whom I had guessed, in the suddenest wild start from sleep, the sleep within my sleep, to be making for my place of rest. The triumph of my impulse, perceived in a flash as I acted on it by myself at a bound, forcing the door outward, was the grand thing, but the great point of the whole was the wonder of my final recognition. Routed, dismayed, the tables turned upon him by my so surpassing him for straight aggression and dire intention, my visitant was already but a diminished spot in the long perspective, the tremendous, glorious hall, as I say, over the far-gleaming floor of which, cleared for the occasion of its great line of priceless vitrines down the middle, he sped for *his* life, while a great storm of thunder and lightning played through the deep embrasures of high windows at the right.

The dread and triumph of his secret mind had fixed itself upon this scene and given it an inexplicable personal reference. (Compare, also, the relationship of the dream to the story *The Jolly Corner*.) It is a proof of James' perfection in his art, an art of suggestion and restraint, that he would attempt no explanation. He superimposed upon the scene of childish awakening the adult dream, his "most appalling yet most admirable nightmare," a dream of an alternation of resistance and pursuit; and could be confident of its effective, sensuous comment upon the whole.

This is an extraordinary swelling of the grain of substance in size and meaning. Memory had enlarged and made valuable a small, definite date of the past while the metaphorical sense had transformed that same bit of substance into a scene standing for an even larger significance. It is, indeed, a singular affair to make of a little boy's first visit to a famous museum.

It is also perfectly characteristic of James to have found his inspiration in a museum, a man-made place, out of the way of man's ordinary, sweated existence. It is just as characteristic that the inspiration he found there should be genuine. The episode outlines his limitations as well as his extraordinary and unique genius. For the reference to be derived from these pages is valid far beyond the scope of the incident. The limitation is of occasion, not of quality.

James showed too, in these passages describing his visits to the crowded museum halls, how, for him, it was necessary that the swirl and rush of two currents should meet to form the artist's proper tension: one of art and one of life. The extraordinary epitomizing quality of this experience was that the idea of the living was as important as that of the making.

It was not just a matter of pictures upon the wall. For the boy as for the man, the spectacle of life, of the inchoate raw material beating upon his senses, was primary, thrilling, and important. This was the stuff which art was to touch and transform. He saw the art in life. Life was his caldron, or was to be. The objects, places, persons, and all their mixed natures were to be his playthings. The child, without words, without ideas, could yet yearn toward these things, these playthings, with a mute and aching responsiveness; toward buildings, streets, the quays, and the river, all the city sights and sounds and smells which he encountered upon his daily exploratory walks.

The remembering of the adventure of the museum was as much a matter of the walks as of any other part of it: of the going "across the Champs-Élysées to the river, and so over the nearest bridge and the quays of the left bank to the Rue de Seine, as if it somehow held the secret of our future"; of passing along

the further quays, with their innumerable old bookshops and print-shops, the long cases of each of these commodities, exposed on the parapets in especial, must have come to know us almost as well as we knew them; with plot thickening and emotion deepening steadily, however, as we mounted the long, black Rue de Seine—*such* a stretch of perspective, *such* an intensity of tone as it offered in those days; where every low-browed vitrine waylaid us and we moved in a world of which the dark message, expressed in we couldn't have said what sinister way too, might have been "Art, art, art, don't you see? Learn, little gaping pilgrims, what *that* is!"

Style looked at him from the buildings along the way, "high grey-headed, clear-faced, straight-standing old houses"; and from the very paving over which he walked, "cobbled and a little grass-grown." He had looked at pictures but he had also "looked at France and looked at Europe, looked even at America as Europe itself might be conceived so to look, looked at history, as a still-felt past and a complacently personal future, at society, manners, types, characters, possibilities and prodigies and mysteries. . . ." The figure of speech he used to characterize his response to this city life was the sensuous one, that of the cat rubbing itself against a piece of furniture; so his "young sensibility felt itself almost rub, for endearment and consecration."

Reflection, experience, the savoring of a memory caused the old man to think of the museum in his personal, symbolizing way. He saw in it a picture to signify the two aspects of his work:

The beginning in short was with Géricault and David, but it went on and on and slowly spread; so that one's stretched, one's even strained, perceptions, one's discoveries and extensions piece by piece, come back, on the great premises, almost as so many explorations of the house of life, so many circlings and hoverings round the image of the world. I have dim reminiscences of permitted independent visits, uncorrectedly juvenile though I might still be, during which the house of life and the palace of art became so mixed and interchangeable . . . that an excursion to look at pictures would have but half expressed my afternoon.

"The house of life and the palace of art"—thus he named his domain. The image of the lonely, excited child exploring the halls of art and of life carries as well the suggestion of the artist's wandering in his adult maze of living and doing. James believed that the artist was alone. Philosophically, as well as artistically, James, in fact, found himself alone. His work has the limitation as well as the advantage of that fact. It has no support in any authority. It makes reference to no system. The richness and complexity of his created world are altogether the result of the operation of a fine and flexible individuality.

He was himself a character fit for his great theme. His private adventure in the great, organized society of his time was the kind of story he liked to tell. It was the story of a sensibility and a character shaped by that world, injured by it and strengthened by it, yet holding onto its integrity; and in some way leaving that world a little different for the encounter.

Bibliographical Note

THE PROPER STUDY OF HENRY JAMES IS THE STUDY OF HIS FIC-
tion. I used both the New York edition of 1908 and the
London edition of 1923 to encompass all, or almost all, of the
fiction which James published during his lifetime. The New
York edition represents the writer's selection for which he wrote
the prefaces. The London edition represents all the fiction
present in the earlier edition in addition to all the previously
published fiction of the author which the editors could gather
together. The text of the London edition duplicates that of the
New York edition where the material is the same; otherwise, it
is the original, unrevised text, as first published by James. The
New York edition was enlarged in 1917, after James' death, to
include his two unfinished novels. Both editions are necessary
to the reader who wants the entire range of the fiction at his
disposal. The two short works listed separately do not appear in
either of the collections. *The Story of a Year,* possibly James'
first published story (1865), was rediscovered and reprinted
recently. *Covering End,* while printed as a story, is a converted
play—*The High Bid.*

The Novels and Tales of Henry James, New York edition. New
York, Charles Scribner's Sons, 1907–1917. 26 volumes.

The Novels and Stories of Henry James, new and complete edition.
London, Macmillan & Co., Ltd., 1923. 35 volumes.

"Covering End," in *The Two Magics.* New York, The Macmillan
Co., 1920.

"The Story of a Year," in *The American Novels and Stories of
Henry James,* edited, and with an introduction, by F. O. Matthiessen.
New York, Alfred A. Knopf, 1947.

For information about James' life, I have relied primarily upon the writer's own word. However partial that word was, however transforming the action of his imagination, yet the author's word was for my purpose the important word. For I was interested in the life only in its bearing upon the fiction. The works listed below contain James' memories of his childhood, his youth, and his first sight of Europe as an interested adult. There are particular memories of his father Henry James, Sr., his brother William, and his cousin Mary Temple. The third volume in order of composition, *The Middle Years*, was to have been concerned with his life as an operative as well as a receptive intelligence, but it breaks off unfinished. Together, the three volumes constitute the writer's own history of the growth of his imagination.

The Middle Years. New York, Charles Scribner's Sons, 1917.
Notes of a Son and Brother. New York, Charles Scribner's Sons, 1914.
A Small Boy and Others. New York, Charles Scribner's Sons, 1913.

As to Henry James' very full and interesting ideas on writing, and on the connections between writing and living, I have found them scattered throughout his nonfiction: in reviews, formal critical essays, travel sketches, and elsewhere. I have made full use of them and have been grateful for them. Such ideas are explicit in the works listed below where they are implicit in the fiction.

The American Scene. New York and London, Harper & Brothers, 1907.
"The Art of Fiction," in *American Critical Essays, XIX–XX Century*, edited, and with an introduction, by Norman Foerster. London, Oxford University Press, 1930. (Reprinted from *Partial Portraits*. The Macmillan Co., 1888.)
English Hours. Boston, Houghton Mifflin Co., 1905.
A Little Tour in France. Boston, Houghton Mifflin Co., 1900.
Notes on Novelists with Some Other Notes. New York, Charles Scribner's Sons, 1914.
Views and Reviews, now first collected (by Le Roy Phillips). Boston, The Ball Publishing Co., 1908. A limited edition.

I list below material of two kinds, both published for the first time since the writer's death, or compiled since that time for easy availability. One kind, including the volumes by Alice and William James, and the books by Elizabeth Robins and Edith Wharton, provides the invaluable, first-hand, biographical comment of sister, brother, or friend. The second type of material, including letters, notebooks, and various scattered papers, helps to round out Henry James' description of himself, a partly conscious and partly unconscious portrait of great value. In addition the work of these writers has preserved writing which in its own right deserves to be preserved.

James, Alice, *Alice James, Her Brothers—Her Journal*, edited, and with an introduction, by Anna Robeson Burr. New York, Dodd, Mead and Co., 1934.

James, Henry, *The Letters of Henry James,* selected and edited by Percy Lubbock. New York, Charles Scribner's Sons, 1920. 2 volumes.

James, Henry, *Letters to A. C. Benson and Auguste Monod,* now first published and edited with an introduction by E. F. Benson. London, Mathews, 1930.

James, Henry, *The Notebooks of Henry James,* edited by F. O. Matthiessen and Kenneth B. Murdock. New York, Oxford University Press, 1947.

James, Henry, *Henry James, Representative Selections,* by Lyon N. Richardson. New York, American Book Co., 1941.

James, William, *The Letters of William James,* edited by his son Henry James. Boston, The Atlantic Monthly Press, 1920. 2 volumes.

Matthiessen, F. O., *The James Family, Including Selections from the Writings of Henry James, Senior, William, Henry, and Alice James.* New York, Alfred A. Knopf, 1947.

Robins, Elizabeth, *Theatre and Friendship: Some Henry James Letters,* with a commentary. New York, G. P. Putnam's Sons, 1932.

Wharton, Edith Newbold (Jones), *A Backward Glance.* New York, D. Appleton–Century Co., Inc., 1934.

The extended passage from Alfred North Whitehead in Part 5, "Attitudes," belongs to the work listed below:

Whitehead, Alfred North, *The Aims of Education, and other Essays.* New York, The Macmillan Co., 1929, pp. 28–30.

Index

167